WINNING

Gaining and Sustaining Victory in the Battles of Life

FEMI MONEHIN

ISBN: 978-1-6847-0461-3 (sc)
ISBN: 978-1-6847-0463-7 (hc)
ISBN: 978-1-6847-0462-0 (e)

Library of Congress Control Number: 2019907098

Lulu Publishing Services rev. date: 06/18/2019

PREFACE

Professional Footballers earn Hundreds of Thousands of Dollars per week. Now can you imagine in a Champions League final match where a striker (a player whose main objective is to score goals) says to his coach, "can you tell the opposing team to stop shoving, pulling and tackling me. Can't they just allow me easy passage and let me put the ball in their net?" If the coach is nice, he will say "you have to score regardless of the tackles and 'attacks' on you...that's why we pay you that much money". He is paid that much to get the ball through the opponents and into the opponent's net. Guess what? The opponents are paid to stop him from scoring. You are rewarded for the victory you orchestrate, either for yourself or for others. Be rest assured that there are people whose rewards are tied to stopping you. That's the reality of life.

You mean there are people out there determined to stop me? Correct. You will find this true in every area of life. In business for instance, the more paying customers (market share) you have the better for you. But guess what, your competitors exist to deplete your market share and increase theirs. Your success is their failure and their success is your failure. It's war. That's just how it is. The same applies to your career, personal life, etc.

Many of us struggle to apply this truth in our personal lives and destiny. You have a destiny to fulfill. Your destiny is not just about the destination; it's all about the journey. Believe it or not you have an enemy whose assignment is to distract, derail or discontinue your journey. Your enemy's name is satan and he has his demon spirits working with him. Therefore, the archenemy of your life and destiny is satan and his demons. However, the truth is that there are people that are consciously or unconsciously aligned with satan and his demons to stop you. Therein lies one of the mysteries of the life of a Christian. You must love these people, BUT you must see them for what they are: enemies.

Jesus said: "Love your enemies..." (Matthew 5:44, NIV). Love them, but they are your enemies. The fact that you love them does not make them your friends. Many have jeopardized their destinies by confusing enemies for friends. *If you can place people correctly, you will win in life.* Too many tragedies are as a result of confusing an enemy for a friend. Once you have succeeded in identifying the enemy, then you can focus on conquering the enemy.

This book will equip you to conquer and win in life.

This has nothing to do with your personality. Some say; "you know I'm not a competitive person", or "I really don't like fighting" or "I just want to mind my business". I understand that. However, the reality of life is that you have people that their life goal is to get an advantage of or to destroy you (your life, business, marriage, children, etc...). Some people are rewarded for stopping you. They will not rest until you are depleted. You must stop them.

One of the greatest damages we can do to the next generation is to pamper them into thinking that conflict is a bad thing; that you can get promoted without passing an examination, that you can get a medal without winning a tournament, that you can obtain victory without fighting battles. God tells us in clear terms that we will have opposition and His expectation is that we will prevail and dominate in spite of the opposition.

Psalm 110:2b (NKJV) "Rule in the midst of your enemies!"

As humans, we have a natural aversion to pain. We just don't like pain. I'm sure you don't. I don't. A man takes his son to the hospital and the son says, "Dad, you won't allow the nurse to hurt me, would you?" the man's heart breaks, but he knows what the son does not know. When the nurse inserts the injection in the little boy's butts, the boy feels the pain and lets out a loud scream and tries to run away, but his father holds him down. He looks at his father with that look… "How could you?" At this point, the tears that roll down the little boy's eyes is not just from the pain of the needle, but the "betrayal" of his dad. Nonetheless, the father knows that he needs to hold the boy down to receive the injection otherwise the sickness will get worse and he may eventually lose his son. The father knows what the son does not know. You may feel that God is "holding you down" for the needles. You may feel the pain of the injection. Like the father in this story, it is uncomfortable for God, but He knows what we don't know: the injection will make us better. The pain is for our gain. We become stronger. Over 2,000 years ago, Jesus hung on the cross with the sin of the whole world. He felt the pain. He felt the "betrayal" of The Father. He shouted, "my Father, my Father, why have you forsaken me" (Matthew 27:46, NLT). The Father turned His face from His beloved Son knowing that *the necessary pain is for the greater good.* Jesus was conflicted, so will we. He felt the pain, so will we. He prevailed & sustained His victory, so should we.

You are the general of your life. It is up to you if you will fulfill your destiny or not. You call the shots. It's your call.

I know some people reading this will disagree and say, "Jesus is the General of my life…" Great. I know. However, God will not force you to do many things, and those things directly affect your destiny. For instance, when it comes to your relationship with Jesus, which determines where you will spend eternity (I don't know anything more important than that) Jesus says "I stand at the door and knock, if anyone opens the door I will come in…"(Revelations 3:20, NIV) Why doesn't He just break down the door? Why does He wait on us to open the door? He does this because He respects our free-will to say "yes" or "no" to Him, He created you to be the General of your life.

It is your call. If it is going to be, then it is up to you. One of the greatest things that happened to me in my walk with God is coming to the realization that God has a great plan for me and that I have a huge, obligatory part to play for that preferred future to become reality. If it is going to be, then it is up to me! God has done and will do His part. You cannot do God's part and He will not do your part. I want to challenge you to do this everyday until it is engrained in you; stand in front of the mirror and say, "if it is going to be, then it is up to me." You can't blame anyone.

You can't blame your parents. You can't blame your circumstances. You can't blame your country or the economy. Everything that happened to you is the past. You cannot change your past. Your past to a large extent gave birth to your present. However, what you do from NOW will give birth to your future. One way to make sure the past determines your future is to keep blaming. Stop blaming. Start fighting for that preferred future. You are the General of your life. Take charge. Stop playing the "blame game" and bring on your "A" game.

The world is waiting for you. Heaven is waiting for you. We all are waiting for you. Bring it on!

You may say "OK, now I want to win, I want to fight, I want victory, but how?" That's a very good question. That's the purpose of this book, to give you WINNING tools and strategy to gain & sustain victory.

ACKNOWLEDGEMENTS

No meaningful achievement in life is really a one-man accomplishment and wrivting a book is not an exception. Writing is a collaborative effort. No good book can be written without the effort and contribution of others.

Therefore, I want to say THANK YOU to the following:

Thank You Holy Spirit!

To my wife Damilola Monehin, thank you. For the support and particularly for allowing me to be away for countless hours at the library in order to write and finish this project, mostly during my vacations ("work-ations").

To my daughter Tehillah, thank you. This book is yours. I pray you learn the principles shared herein and become the great person God has made you to be.

To my grandmother "mama" and my mum (Dr. Mrs. R.A. Monehin), the matriarchs that imparted priceless wisdom into me, thank you!

To my ever cooperative and hardworking editor, Debbie Dimowo, thank you.

To the best colleagues on the face of the earth; Tolu Osinjolu, Itohan Uwaifo, Hadassah Odianosen, Haruna Ishaya, Juliet Ume, Alfred Nwachukwu and of course, Debbie Dimowo, thank you guys!

To the amazing team at Lulu Publishing; Deb Johnson, Grace Ansell, Jeff Slone and Mary Abarquez (my very first Check in Coordinator), thank you guys!

To God's Favourite House, THANK YOU!

INTRODUCTION

*Spectacular Success Depends On Your Ability To **Think** And To **Act** Strategically*

You are the General of your life. Like any military commander, resounding success depends on your ability to think and act strategically. You call the shots and for the victory to be effected, you must understand that your ability to think and act strategically is indispensable.

I am a student of military campaigns and warfare. Careful studies of historic and modern-day military campaigns reveal universal principles crucial for every battlefield victory and every great General utilize these specific strategies to ensure victory.

The research of great military campaigns has revealed universal principles crucial for every battlefield victory. The principles are so universal that nations that disagree on political positions and social formation utilize the same principles when it comes to military engagements. No matter how far apart their philosophies are, they all utilize these principles; the Russians use it, the Chinese use it, the Americans use it, the British use it, Ancient African warriors use it and the Jews are masters at it. In fact, as you will discover, these principles are rooted in the Bible. It appears that these great generals learned it from the Bible.

Life is a battle. Face it. You don't need to spend a long time on earth to discover this truth. At birth the baby becomes restless in the womb and desires to experience the outside world. Yet the baby has to fight and break through. Everyone reading this book was in the womb at a point in time. You fought and broke through. You may not know it, but there is fight in you. Unleash it! You are a winner. You are a victor. Let's go back a little bit to before the baby was formed in the mother's womb. When the father's sperms are released into the mother, there are tens of millions of sperm cells, with each racing to get to the egg first. It's a contest. Only one sperm wins and fertilizes the egg. Only one! Out of tens of millions. Guess what, in your mother's case, YOU ARE THE ONE! You are the winner! You are one in a million. You fought. The terrain was challenging, but you persevered. There were millions contesting for your egg, but you prevailed. You were born a champion. A winner. A victor. Winning is in you!

As we grow up, we seem to forget this very truth about ourselves and about the realities of life. Life is a battle, a contest. It is war. Guess what? You have what it takes to win; you already proved that at birth. It's in you. You are the general of your life. Every war is propagated by Generals and you are the general of your life? You call the shots.

In this book, you will learn The Twelve Principles of Military Engagements. There are actually more than twelve principles, but the twelve presented in this book are the foundation of all military strategy.

It doesn't matter whether you are a businessperson, an entrepreneur, a solo-preneur, a freelancer, a professional or a stay at home mom. Deploying these principles will save your life and guarantee victory.

You are the General of your life. In battle, the general is responsible for calling the shots. You are responsible for your life; your father is not, your mother is not, your siblings are not, your friends are not, your boss is not, your pastor is not, your rabbi is not, your country is not, YOU ARE RESPONSIBLE FOR YOUR LIFE. Therefore, achieving victory in every facet of your life is greatly dependent on your ability to think and to act strategically. This is indispensable. Spectacular success depends on your ability to think and act strategically.

Each chapter deals with a specific principle. Enjoy!

CHAPTER 1
THE PRINCIPLE OF THE OBJECTIVE

The Objective: "Direct all efforts towards a clearly defined, decisive and attainable objective."

He That Has No Plan Will Always Succumb To He That Has A Plan

Every war is propagated by an objective. Unfortunately, not many people engage with a clear objective. A lot of people go through life just hoping that things will turn out well. But we see in Scripture that that is not how God deals. God always starts with the end in mind. He always starts with an objective.

The first principle of war is the principle of the objective. What is the vision? What is the objective? Once you're clear on the objective, then direct ALL effort towards realizing it. Always start with a clearly defined objective. Remember, "Where there is no vision [an objective], the people perish" Prov. 29:18 (KJV, emphasis added). *Never forget that he that has no plan will always succumb to he that has a plan*. This truth is applicable across board; in marriage for instance, you must have a plan for your spouse. If the wife has no plan to keep the husband happy, guess what will happen? The strange woman always has a plan on how to keep your husband happy. Guess who would win? This is not an attempt to prophesy evil but merely to show you the power of having an objective.

The sad reality is that Christians do not like the truth. This is the truth; he that has a plan will always prevail over he that does not have a plan. What is your plan to keep your wife super loved in your marriage relationship? What is your plan to keep your husband extremely happy and to make him feel like a king in his house? What is your plan to make your spouse totally satisfied in all areas? The reality is that if you do not have a plan, someone else does, and he that has a plan will always prevail. What is your plan to crush your business competitors? What is your plan to make your employees fulfilled at work? What is your plan for your boss? What is the objective?

I am an advocate for goal setting especially for believers. Identify key areas in your life and draw up a plan [goals] for them. You must have clear-cut objectives. Come up with physical goals, material goals, leisure goals, emotional goals, and developmental goals.

Stop and ask yourself "what is the objective?" Ask this question in every area of your life; in your business, before entering any partnership, in your career, in your finances, in your marriage, etc. What is the objective? What is the goal? What is the plan?

The person that has a plan will always prevail over the person that doesn't. What is your plan? If you do not have a plan, someone else has a plan for you.

God wants you to have victory; consistent, sustained and repeatable victory. But victory does not happen by chance. Victory does not happen haphazardly. If by some stroke of luck, one were to stumble on victory without knowing how, chances are that it will just be a flash in the pan. It will just be luck. You will not be able to sustain nor repeat it.

However, understanding the principles of war equips every general with the ability to reproduce victory notwithstanding the location, the opposition, or the terrain; through deliberate action, strategic thinking, spiritual effort, unprecedented favour and daring courage. If by understanding the principles of war you gained victory in a certain location, then you find yourself facing another opposition in another location or terrain, guess what's going to happen? You will gain victory again. Your victory will be repeatable because the first one was not by chance. The first one was by deliberate action, strategic thinking, spiritual effort, unprecedented favour and daring courage. As a student of military campaigns and warfare, I have discovered that throughout history no great general goes into battle without a clear objective.

About 331BC, there was a king called Dairus III. He was in charge of Persia. And there was a young Macedonian general called Alexandria the Great. Alexandria the Great was just 25 years old and he was notorious for conquering kingdoms and taking territories. Dairus, the king of Persia had 200,000 infantry lined up. Alexander had 50,000 soldiers but Alexandra had a plan. Dairus' security was in his numbers, but Alexandra had an objective. He allowed king Dairus to capture some of his men knowing fully well that Dairus will torture the men for intelligence. Sure enough, Dairus tortured the men until they began to confess, and they gave Dairus wrong information. They told Dairus that Alexandra was set to attack hat night. So Dairus set up his entire army for battle and they waited all night long meaning they did not get any sleep. Alexandra set up a few of his men to shoot arrows at different intervals in the night just to prep up the enemy's array while he allowed 99% of his soldiers to rest all through the night. And by morning, Dairus' soldiers were tired but Alexandra's soldiers were sharp and ready for battle. Alexandra's plan is not to hide his identity. He would always show up to battle dressed in shining armor, his helmet adorned with jewels, and riding on his black horse. So he is visible to everyone in his camp and to everyone in the enemy's camp. His 50,000 men had one objective; attack the flanks, create space in the center for Alexandra to ride straight through and kill the king of the opposition. Once Alexandra is able to kill the king of the opposing side or gets him to run, the battle is more or less over. This plan sounds really simple right? But it is a plan. Dairus was putting up a fight but Alexandra implemented his plan. The flanks opened up, he rode straight through and struck Dairus. The 200,000 soldiers fled. The Persians recorded 90,000 soldiers dead. Alexander had only 50 soldiers dead.

What was the difference? One person had an objective while the other person was hoping things would turn out right. Do not leave your life to chance! What is your objective? You know, God can have a sense of humor. Alexandra conquered so many territories. However, he died of malaria on his way back from India. God brought down Alexandra the great with an ordinary mosquito. Fear God!

There is another interesting story...this time from the Bible, the book of Joshua chapter 6. It is the story of Israel. God had given them a clear objective for taking the city Jericho. (I suggest you read the story if you are not familiar with it). The instruction was clear: surround the city once on one day. Do that for seven days. On the seventh day, surround it seven times. On the seventh time blast the trumpet, once the people hear the blast of the trumpet the walls will come down. Guess what Jericho did? As big as Jericho was, as fortified as their wall was, as advanced in military warfare as they were, they chose to sit back and defend. You need to know this: sit and defend does not guarantee victory. The wall of Jericho was so thick, they built houses on the wall. As the people of Israel were walking round the city, they had an objective. The people of Jericho must have concluded the Jews were crazy after watching them walk round the wall on day one, day two, day three...

Sometimes when you are in pursuit of your objective, you look like a fool. You have to be comfortable with that. It's okay to look like a fool, at the end of the day we will know who is the fool. The king of Jericho must have sent people to check what was going on. Are they looking for holes in the wall? Are they looking for the entrance or what? But by the seventh day, they matched round seven times, they blasted the ram's horns, they shouted and the walls came crashing down. Israel charged into the city and took a city greater than them. This, my friend, is the power of having an objective. It is so indispensable.

Now that we are clear on what an objective is and have explained the huge significance of having one. Let's take another look at the principle of The Objective. In military strategy, the principle of **The Objective** states thus: "Direct **all efforts** towards a clearly defined, decisive and attainable objective." So, you have a clearly defined objective, and it is decisive and attainable. The next thing to do is **direct all efforts** towards it.

What does victory look like? What is the objective? When you look at your business, what does victory look like? How does it look? What is your objective? Direct **ALL EFFORTS** in that direction. In your relationship with your spouse, what does victory look like? Direct all efforts in that direction. What is that picture of victory in your health? Direct all efforts in that direction. What does victory look like in your finances? Direct all efforts in that direction.

Three key things that must be in place before we should deploy all our effort: Direct all efforts towards a **clearly defined**, **decisive**, and **attainable** objective.

ATTAINABLE

If Your Vision Does Not Require A Supernatural Intervention, Your Vision Is Too Small

Do not shoot for something that is not attainable. Do not waste your time and resources on things that are not attainable. You could be wondering "are we not supposed to believe God for the big things and the things that are not humanly possible?" Yes, we are. So, I say, always make allowance for the 1 Corinthians 2:9 [NIV] "clause" in your vision – "What no eye has seen, no ear has heard, and no mind has imagined…" And these things always look totally unattainable. While your vision should make provision for the unimaginable, however, your individual goals should be attainable. A vision can look totally ridiculous & unattainable. That's OK. If your vision does not require supernatural intervention, your vision is too small. What is the vision for that organization that you are leading? What is the vision for that business? What is the vision for your family and for your children? If it does not require supernatural intervention, then it is too small.

However, when you define an objective, it is important that it is attainable. Again, do not waste your time and resources on non-attainable objectives. Now let us bring this home with an illustration. Alexandra the great, for instance, had a vision to conquer the world. That definitely sounds ridiculous. However, to achieve that vision, he needs to conquer every nation on earth and one of such nations at the time was Persia. So, he must come up with a clearly defined, decisive and attainable objective of conquering Persia, and he did. Another example is this: most people are looking to lose weight these days. In fact, so many people are obsessed with losing weight. So, a young man decides that he is going to lose 20kg in two weeks. If you actually lose 20kg in two weeks, I would be worried and would probably pray for you. It is unhealthy and in most cases, it is unattainable. That young man is putting himself under unnecessary pressure. He is going to feel like a failure if after two weeks he hasn't lost 20kg simply because he has set an unrealistic goal for himself. He can actually lose 20kg in 3 months. It is a tough goal, but it is attainable.

DECISIVE

FOCUS: Follow One Course Until Success.

General Karl Von Clausewitz (a Prussian general and military theorist) captures this entire thought aptly, "*Pursue one great decisive aim with force and determination.*" The problem most of the time comes from pursuing different things. They say if you chase three rabbits at the same time, you will catch none. Pursue **one** decisive aim with force and determination. Ask yourself "What is that one thing in this field that must be done?" Pursue it with vigor. Robert Kiyosaki, one of the hosts of a podcast I listen to, shared his acronym for focus and I really liked it. He said, to focus is to Follow One Course Until Successful. A lot of people are in the habit of abandoning a course as soon as they encounter an obstacle. Obstacles are part of the process, get used to it. One of the fastest destroyers is indecision. When we dillydally, we rob ourselves of significant progress. Be decisive. Don't waver. Follow one course until success. How long do you want to start this and stop this, or start that and stop that? Don't be like water. Water always flows through the path of least resistance. When water is flowing, it always dodges obstacles. People that are like water in this respect cannot bare the heat that comes with greatness.

Follow one course until success. Take business for instance, no one succeeds in business by being passive. No business succeeds by being passive. One passive activity businesses engage in is cost cutting. The truth is that no business becomes great just by cutting costs. Cutting costs is putting yourself on a back-foot. It is necessary sometimes and it is important that you do. However, if that is your focus as a business leader (or a church leader or political leader), that enterprise is not going anywhere. At best it will be in survival mode. If you must cut costs, then let other people focus on that. You focus on taking the business to the next level. Focus on the objective as the leader. You are the general, focus on the objective. Brian Tracy says, "Businesses succeeds because of high sales; businesses fail because of low sales, everything else is complimentary." Even a school owner is a sales person. You either sell that school or the school goes down and the only person that can drive that sales is you the point person. You are the general. Josh.1:8 "Keep this Book of the Law always on your lips; meditate on it day and night, so that you may be careful to do everything written in it. Then you will be prosperous and successful." (NIV). You can replace the phrase *careful to do* with one word – decisive.

CLEARLY DEFINED

Clarity Comes From **God Speaking** And From **Clear Thinking**

Make it clear, make it simple. If you read Joshua 6:2-5 [NLT] God was crystal clear. *"2 But the Lord said to Joshua, "I have given you Jericho, its king, and all its strong warriors. 3 You and your fighting men should march around the town once a day for six days. 4 Seven priests will walk ahead of the Ark, each carrying a ram's horn. On the seventh day you are to march around the town seven times, with the priests blowing the horns. 5 When you hear the priests give one long blast on the rams' horns, have all the people shout as loud as they can. Then the walls of the town will collapse, and the people can charge straight into the town."* (Joshua 6:2-5. NLT) God communicated His instructions clearly to the children of Israel. It does not get clearer than this. Strive for clarity in all things. When I read the instructions that the U.S. General Eisenhower gave during World War II, I was intrigued by the clarity. His instruction was; *"proceed to London, occupy Europe, get rid of the Germans."* Crystal clear instruction. Many times, because we are not clear, we are busy doing things that are not necessary. Benjamin Tregoe captures it rather aptly when he says, "The very worst use of time is to do something well that need not be done at all." You are sitting for an algebra examination. Obviously, scores are going to be awarded based on your knowledge of algebra. But you get into the examination hall, and you decide to respond to the questions based on your knowledge of theory of statistics. So, you abandon the algebra question and pour down statistics because you are aiming to impress. This is a class example of wasting time to do well something that needed not be done at all. The worst use of time is to do something well that need not be done at all. Seek clarity with all your might. Time spent in getting clarity is time well spent. What's the hurry when you are not clear?

Clarity is key! Seek clarity with all your might. If you have clarity on any issue, you can confront the issue with confidence. Many times however, life can seem like an unsolvable puzzle. So how do you get clarity in life? Clarity comes from two sources; clarity comes from God speaking and from clear thinking. You need to devout time to clear thinking. A lot of the time, we are seeking God's face and asking Him to speak. Yes, God speaks, and we are totally grateful for that. But sometimes God wants you to think. You are saying, "God speak your servant is listening." But God is saying, "No, you think, your God is waiting!" You must know the difference. I understand the place of asking and there is a place for asking because God instructs us to ask until our joy is full. But you and I must be able to tell the difference particularly when God is leading us to think. I once had a peculiar experience relating to this subject. It was during a period when there was scarcity of petrol in Lagos, Nigeria. I hate it when there is scarcity of petrol and for any one that has experienced it, I am sure they hate it too. I was on the queue at a station that was selling. Even though I could see the gate of the filing station from my position on the queue, the queue itself was moving very slowly. Across the road, on the other side of the expressway, I could see the filing station there also selling. Naturally, I began to inquire of the Lord, you would be amazed at the things I ask the Holy Spirit. I said, "Please speak to your boy; should I stay on this queue or should I go across to the other petrol station?" I did not get any response from the Lord. I said, "Speak Lord, Your boy is waiting." Still no response so I continued to press in and what the Holy Spirit said to me shocked me. He said, "Use your brain!" Use my brain? Oh yes, I have a brain. So, I analyzed the situation. This filing station closes early and the queue is not moving fast. Even though I am already on the queue, I probably would not get a chance to buy petrol before the station closes. However, the filing station across the road closes late, even though the queue there is longer, I have a better chance of buying petrol there. So, I got out of the queue and went to the filing station across the express. While driving home after buying petrol, I saw the car that was in front of me at the previous station parked outside the gate of the filling station and the gate was locked. **Use your brain!**

Check; are you waiting for God to speak meanwhile He is actually waiting for you to think? Clear thinking is so powerful. The problem is that a lot of us are so consumed with certainty rather than clarity. Clarity is different from certainty. You can be clear without being certain. We worry so much about being certain. Some people never want to take action until they are certain. If you always wait until you are certain to take action, it will be too late. All you need is clarity not certainty. For instance, when I got clarity with my thinking, I knew I needed to go to the petrol station across the expressway. Was I certain I was going to buy petrol? No! Was I clear that that was what I was supposed to do? Yes! Clarity is one thing, certainty is another. In fact, uncertainty is a permanent part of life. Most people hate uncertainty. Yet some of us have learned to grow very comfortable in uncertain situations. Uncertainty does not bother me. Rather, I strive for clarity.

I am sorry to break it to you but uncertainty never goes away – never! But while we can afford to be uncertain, we cannot afford to be unclear. I pray that you will receive clarity from heaven in Jesus Name. You need clarity of thought.

The only thing you can be 100% certain about is the past. "But what about faith?" You may ask. "I can be certain about God's Word, right? Didn't the Bible say that, faith is the substance [the certainty] of things hoped for?" I know and if you read the Bible in context you will see that God's Word only brings clarity to 'What'. In most cases, 'How' always remains uncertain. Faith is the substance of the things hoped for – 'what', clarity about 'what'. 'How' mostly, if not always, remains uncertain. Ask Abraham. God told him, "Look at the stars in the heavens so shall your seed be!" [Genesis 15:5, KJV paraphrased]. Did he know 'How'? In fact, Abraham was so uncertain about 'How' that he impregnated his wife's maid. Ask Joseph. It had been revealed to him, he was going to be great and his brothers will bow to him. But he had no clue 'How'. Did he know he was going to go to prison, or be in a pit? Joseph had no clue. Ask David, he had no clue how he was going to ascend the throne. The list goes on and on.

A clear objective eliminates distractions automatically. A clear objective takes out unnecessary options. I admire the late Steve Jobs a lot. Many of us have some of his ideas in our hands. Steve Jobs captures this exact thought really aptly. He says, "I'm actually as proud of the things we haven't done as the things we have done. Innovation is saying no to 1,000 things." The only reason why he is able to say "no" to this good idea and that good idea is because he has an objective to say "yes" to one great idea. This has saved us a lot in pastoring. There are so many opportunities to go in different directions. We should be doing this, and we should be doing that. We are able to say no because we have a very clear objective. When my colleagues need to make a decision on a project or a direction, I say to them, if it is not a triple "yes" then it is a "no". If there is a project before you and you are wondering if you should pursue it or not. My advice is, if it is not a triple "yes" then it is a "no". Why? The reason is that if it is not a triple "yes", then it will be average. The fact that something is good in not enough. Do not make decisions solely based on the fact that something is good enough. Be clear on where it stands as it relates to your objective and move only when it is a triple "yes".

When you say "yes" to Jesus, you automatically are saying "no" to satan, "no" to darkness, "no" to curses, "no" to demons, and "no" to sin. Believe me, that is a beautiful place to be. When you say "yes" to God, you are saying "no" to satan, "no" to oppression, "no" to the manipulation of the enemy. "Where there is no prophetic vision the people cast off restraint." Prov.29:18 (ESV) "If people can't see what God is doing, they stumble all over themselves." Prov.29:18 (NLT) When you see people stumbling, making errors, and they appear to be doing thing upside down. It is because they have lost sight of what God is doing. Whereas, clarity comes from **God Speaking** and from **Clear Thinking**.

Ask yourself: what is the objective? Make sure it is clearly defined, decisive and attainable. Then direct all effort towards achieving it.

CHAPTER 2
THE PRINCIPLE OF THE OFFENSIVE

The Offensive: "Advance and attack the opposition. Grab and exploit the opportunities."

Every Force That Is On The Offensive Mostly Prevails Over The Defensive Force

Having an objective is one thing, execution is another thing entirely. The ability to execute is a major differentiator between the average and the great person. What is the purpose of having an objective if you will not get up and make it happen?

Now that you have set a clear objective, move forward. Advance. Begin to attack, to grab, to seize, and to exploit opportunities. A lot of Christians are passive; they are just sitting and waiting around for a miracle to happen. You cannot just be waiting around for heaven to do something. The **Principle of The Offensive** is advance and attack the opposition. Grab and exploit the opportunities. God is saying you have to advance, you have to attack, you have to seize, and you have to grab the opportunities. Why? It is up to you to exploit every opportunity that God presents. God won't do that for you.

The story is told of two friends, Musa and Kamoru, that both went to visit the oracle to foretell how things will be by the end of the agricultural year. The oracle told Musa, "The year is financially bright for you. I see that you are going to be very wealthy by the end of this agricultural year." Musa began to dance and rejoice. The same oracle turned to Kamoru and said, "This year is going to be financially gloomy for you. You are going to have a bad year. I see that you are going to be very poor by the end of this agricultural year." Kamoru was understandably very sad. On their way home, Kamoru said to his friend Musa "I have no business believing the oracle. I already have an objective to expand my farm and secure a huge harvest." To which Kamoru replied, "Well, I am so believing the oracle. My future is great. This is going to be a great year. Don't worry I will take care of you since we are friends." So, they went their separate ways. Kamoru decided to believe in his objective and not the words of the oracle, so he worked really hard. His execution was with vigor. He expanded his farm, worked the soil, fought the pests, catered for his workmen, spent several extra hours working towards his objective, grabbing and exploiting every opportunity that came his way. Musa on the other hand printed out the words of the oracle in very large fonts and placed it in his living room, displayed it everywhere on his farm and in his home. He made his wife and children confess it twice everyday. However, Musa took every opportunity not to work. He slept early, woke up late, would not put in the hard work. He refused to be answerable to anyone. Anytime Kamoru comes to visit and his wife mentions it, Musa becomes all-defensive. If Kamoru presses further to discuss it with him, Musa was quick to remind him of what the oracle said about him and suggests that Kamoru was jealous of him. So Kamoru left him alone and focused on his work. Though there were several attempts by the weather, pests and thieves to erode his harvest, Kamoru fought back really hard. He refused to be reduced to penury. He overcame terrible weather, destructive pests and stealing workmen. When it was time for harvest, Musa had nothing to harvest as pest and bad weather had destroyed most of his harvest. The ones not destroyed by the weather and pests, were stolen by deceitful workmen. He had no harvest. Poverty was staring him in the face. Kamoru on the other hand had plentiful harvest. So much he needed to hire extra hands to bring in the harvest. Musa had financial gloom, while Kamoru had financial abundance.

The key lesson here is this: You are the general of your life. If it is going to be, then it is up to you. Until you take action and be on the offensive, nothing changes.

Your destiny is not in anyone's hands. It is not determined by what the oracles say. It is not determined by that the prophets say. You determine it! There are loads of examples of when God himself changes his mind on an issue. If you think the odds are against you, do not give in. You must never say, "What will be will be". You must always say, "What will be is up to me".

You must be on the offensive to actualize your objective. No one is going to drop greatness on your laps. Even if it is dropped on your laps, you need to be on the offensive to preserve it.

In military strategy, the **Principle of The Offensive** states thus: *Advance and attack the opposition. Grab and exploit the opportunities.*

The British Principles of War Book and the US Army Field Manual puts it this way:

"Offensive action is the practical way in which a commander seeks to gain advantage, sustain momentum and seize the initiative." – British Principles of War

"Seize, retain, and exploit the initiative. Offensive action is the most effective and decisive way to attain a clearly defined common objective. Offensive operations are the means by which a military force seizes and holds the initiative while maintaining freedom of action and achieving decisive results. This is fundamentally true across all levels of war." – US Army Field Manual

Offensive action is the primary way a general influences the outcome of a battle. If you don't want to end up like Musa (in the story above), you need to be deliberate and take offensive actions like Kamoru in order to influence and control the outcome. You can't just sit down, hoping things will happen for you. You have to get up and make it happen.

Advance, move forward and begin to attack. Begin to grab. Begin to seize. Begin to exploit opportunities. Don't be passive, don't just sit around waiting for a miracle. We are waiting for heaven to make things happen for us and God is saying to you, "advance, attack, seize, grab the opportunities and exploit".

If you find that you are stagnant or at best going round in circles, you need to deploy the **Principle of The offensive**. It is time to move forward. It is time to move on the offensive. I'm here to challenge you; I'm here to say to you "dare to move forward". Dare to move forward. Dare to take the step. Dare to make progress.

Every move of God is preceded by a trigger, usually a sound. And this is evident and consistent with Scriptures, from Genesis to Revelation. Every time a move of God about to start, there is a trigger, a sound, like a clarion call. For example, Genesis 1:1 (NLT, emphasis added) *"In the beginning God created the heavens and the earth. 2 The earth was formless and empty, and darkness covered the deep waters. And the Spirit of God was hovering over the surface of the waters. 3 Then God said, **"Let there be light…"**"* I *can imagine that at this very moment there was a loud thunderous sound made by God's voice: "Let there be light…" "…and there was light."* 1 Kings 18:41 (KJV) *"And Elijah said unto Ahab, Get thee up, eat and drink; for there is a sound of abundance of rain.".* In this case, Elijah heard a spiritual sound. There must have been a loud thunder clap in the spirit, and then rain began to fall. Acts 2:1 [NLT] *"On the day of Pentecost all the believers were meeting together in one place. 2 Suddenly, there was a sound from heaven like the of a mighty windstorm, and it filled the house where they were sitting"* and the Holy Ghost was released. Take it that God is giving you the sound now, dare to move forward! Attack!

Watching movies of oriental wars has always fascinated me. The infantry and cavalry line up and set in array. The two armies line up facing each other with a gulf in-between them. Each soldier keeping ranks and pumped up for battle. Nothing happens. Everybody is fuming, they're revving as it were. Then all of a sudden, a General shouts "ATTACK". You know what happens next. Everybody plunges forward in frenzy, facing the enemy head-on. God is saying to you "ATTACK". You need to say to yourself "ATTACK". Business is a battle. Marriage is a battle, you're still trying to make your spouse happy meanwhile another person is trying to "put eye inside". Life is a battle. "ATTACK"

You cannot afford to be passive. One of the greatest mistakes you can make is to think, "as long as I'm a good person, I don't have to fight any battle." Life is a battle. Face it.

"War once declared must be waged offensively & aggressively. The enemy must not be fended off; the enemy must be smitten down." -Alfred Mahan

Once the line is drawn, the enemy must not be fended off; the enemy must be smitten down. Listen my friend, action is everything. There are largely two types of people in the world; the 'thinkers' and the 'doers'. It is not that the 'thinkers' do not do or that the 'doers' do not think, but people are predominantly tilted in a certain direction. I have realized that it is easier to get a 'doer' to think, than to get a 'thinker' to do. I will always employ a 'doer' over a 'thinker' (all other things being equal). 'Doers' are action people and you can teach an action person to think. But it is difficult to get a 'thinker' off his or her seat. 'Thinkers' are always analyzing. After they have analyzed, then they reanalyze again and again. Then after that, they will analyze again and again until they get what is called, analysis-paralysis. Action is everything!

The person that commits to continuous action in vigorous pursuit of his or her goal, will always have an advantage over the person that sits down and waits for a "miracle". The person that gets up and executes [take action] will always prevail over the person that sits and waits. I am a believer, do not get me wrong, I believe in miracles. However, even with miracles, there is the God part and there is the man part. You cannot do God's part and God will not do your part. You need to get up on your own two feet and attack. You need to get up and take action, make things happen. I am in love with people that make things happen. I see a lot of philosophers, even in church. They are constantly analyzing things, I listen to them and I move on. I am friendlier with action people.

Napoleon Bonaparte, the great French General captures the need for action aptly when he says, "Opportunities? I **make** opportunities!" In other words, while others choose to sit and wait for opportunities, he is committed to making opportunities. This is someone that by all indications, does not appear to have walked with God. So, what is our excuse as believers? Action is everything.

In the popular battle for Northern part of Africa, the Italians had suffered a huge defeat from the British. The Italians sent word to the Germans to come and help them. The British intelligence of course was up to date, they knew the Germans were coming. But the British calculated that when the German ships arrive, they will first of all birth, then offload their tanks and battle trucks, and set them in array. So, they came up with a plan based on these calculations. But the famous German General Rommel began to dispatch the tanks and battle trucks into battle in waves as soon as the ships birthed. The British were still calculating, they did not know what hit them. Wave after wave after wave, Rommel dealt with the British forces totally and won the war. Not because the British had lesser military capacity, or they lacked the intelligence, or the intelligence was inaccurate but because the Germans were on the offensive. It would have been a different story if the British attacked as soon as the German ships birthed.

Every force that is on the offensive mostly prevails over the defensive force. The defensive force is mostly at the mercy of the offensive force. I like to play sports and some years ago I started playing tennis. I had previously misjudged the sport from a distance as a waste of time. It was when I started playing that I realized how technical a game tennis is. Tennis engages every part of your being. It is like warfare. In my opinion, the greatest players are the attacking players. The prayers that are strong defensively but are able to transition into attack very easy are also very strong players. Novak Djokovic, for example, is one of the best defensive players in the world. He is able to transition very quickly from defense to attack. I have played different players with different and unique styles and skills. I discovered that in a game, the players that I have the most difficulty playing are the attacking players. Players that will keep on hitting the ball even when they are five love down.

Napoleon says, "No great battles are ever won on the defensive." You cannot win on the defensive, you need to be on the offensive. In prayer for instance, you need to be on the offensive. In giving, you need to be on the offensive. In forgiving, you need to be on the offensive. In loving, you need to be on the offensive. Do not wait until the person that offends you asks for forgiveness. Forgive him or her in advance. Be on the offensive! In football [soccer], as long as I can remember, I have always played forward on the wings. As I grew in the game, I began to play as center forward (a striker). I have always loved to attack and to lead counter attacks because that is where the strength of the game is. I have never understood midfielders that pass sideways and backwards. It is irritating to me. The truth is, you do not win matches in your lower third. You win matches by attacking in the upper third. I love to watch the game also; there are teams that will take the ball into the front of their opponent's box eighteen and begin to pass. They do this simply because of this principle, you win matches by attacking. There is another club that will push to get the highest goal count in every game. Meaning if the opposing team scores five goals, they would score six before the game is over. This particular team is not very strong defensively but largely they will score more in any game. Even the teams that were famous for their brazen defense are changing their patterns of play to attack. Why? Simply because you do not win matches defending. You win matches by attacking.

One of the best goal keepers in the world (as at the time of this writing), Manuel Neuer, is an attacking goal keeper. You would think that as a goal keeper, he should be only concerned about defending the goal post. Statistics show that he spends more time outside of his box eighteen than inside. As soon as he gets hold of the ball in a game, his focus is to set his wingers and attackers free. He is sweeping, creating forward movement. There is no nation that wins defensively. There is no army that wins defensively. There is no life that goes forward defensively. There is no career that makes progress defensively. There is no business that gains grounds defensively. You have to attack! One of the masters of attack from military history is a war General, Genghis Khan of the Mongol empire. Genghis Khan's attacking strategy is straight forward; he besieges a city, he divides his large army into three with eight hour shifts each. He attacks the city round the clock. There is no rest or break, he does not waste time on regrouping. There has never been a city that has been able to withstand his attack. He overtook Asia from North Eastern Asia and he spread over the whole of Asia, Middle East even part of Eastern Europe.

The Mongol empire is the largest contiguous Empire in the history of man. The reason for expansion of the Mongol empire was not defense. The reason for expansion is one word and that word is **attack!** It got to a point that cities would willing surrender their city to Genghis Khan in exchange for fair treatment. You could call him a good man because he would only demand for tributes from such cities.

In the spirit realm, prayer puts you on the offensive. I believe this is why Jesus tells us to pray without ceasing. If you are like me, you add fasting to praying for greater results. Attack! Luke 18:1 (NLT) "One day Jesus told his disciples a story to show that they should always pray and never give up…" In this parable, Jesus tells us the story of a woman seeking for justice from an unjust judge. The judge ignores her request at first but the woman continues to attack the judge until one day he cracks and gives her what she wants. And then Jesus says to us in Luke 18:8 (NLT) "I tell you, he will grant justice to them quickly! But when the Son of Man returns, how many will he find on the earth who have **faith**?" [with emphasis]. A lot of people have misjudged the phrase "have faith" to mean a passive thing. But if you read the story that Jesus gave about having faith, you will see that having faith is active, action. It is knocking on that door until the door opens or you break it down. In essence, Jesus is saying when He return, because He will return, will He find people that will not take 'No' for an answer? Will He find people that will understand the objective that God has for them and keep hammering until they get what they want. I say to the Lord, "Look no further, here we are!" We will give all that it takes and we will get a breakthrough. I challenge you to make this same commitment in the different areas of your life. You need to be offensive in prayer.

Be on the offensive in giving. I have had to give my way out of a tight place. Learn to give offensively. You cannot afford to be passive in your giving. It is only offensive giving that gets you out of a tight place. You cannot be passive particularly in the area of giving. Stop waiting for 'someone' to come along and help you out. The person that commits to continuous action in vigorous pursuit of his or her goal, will always have an advantage over the person that sits down and waits for a "miracle". The person that gets up and executes [actions] will always prevail. So many people are given to excuses. The Bible describes it as, 'the lion in the street' story. The common excuse with is that things are hard! My response is, really? How come in this same country people are getting wealthy and it is 100% legitimate? I am sure you know that not every wealthy person attained that status fraudulently. Do not deceive yourself. There are people that are wealthy, and they are on the right path. I know people that do not bribe anybody, and their revenue is amazing. If you keep looking suspiciously at wealthy people and assume they are cheating in some way, you would miss it. Make up your mind today to stop making excuses, instead choose to make progress. You cannot make both excuses and progress at the same time. The oven temperature for excuses is very different from that of progress. It is impossible for your oven to bake excuses and bake progress at the same time. Your oven will choose what it will bake, excuses or progress, what will it be?

George Washington, a great war General and the first president of the United States of America says, "99% of failures come from people who have the habit of making excuses." In any organization, 99% of failures will come from people that will make excuses. There are people that even have research data to back up their excuses for apparent failure. Have you met any of such people? If you run a business, check! Even in your home, check; the children that make the most excuses are the children that never have their assignment, homework, or chores done. You cannot make excuses and make progress at the same time. You have to determine to make progress and I pray that God will back you up all the way, in Jesus Name. One of the marks of truly successful people and of the best war generals is, they take responsibility for their affairs. You are the general of your life. Whether you are in paid employment or running your own business; true success comes when you take responsibility for your affairs. Successful people are full of action, intense, and committed to victory.

One cannot talk about war Generals without talking about David. David was one of the most brilliant war Generals that ever walked the face of the earth and he also got it right with God. In 1 Samuel 17 [NLT], David saw Goliath and challenged him. Goliath cursed David, David cursed Goliath right back. Action is everything – attack! You do not let the enemy have the final say no matter what. Whether it is the enemy within or the enemy without, or even a voice in your head. Respond to every voice that tries to tell you that you cannot make it. Make sure the enemy does not have the final say. If it is an enemy without speaking negatively into your life, respond. The story is told of a lady that loves God passionately and so would not stand for corruption. Her boss was not very pleased with their stand. So, he threatened her that as long as he remains in the organization, she will never be promoted. Her response was, "With all due respect, Sir, I will be promoted." They went back and forth on it for a while. You can tell what happened in the end, he lost his job and she was promoted. You have to answer; you have to have the last say. Regardless of who speaks negatively to you, always respond. Even If it is your parent speaking negatively over you, answer back as respectfully as you can, but respond.

Saul said to David, you cannot kill this Goliath. David answered back, "I will kill him". David gave his reasons, "I killed the bear, I killed the lion, I will kill this Goliath too". Goliath cursed David with his god.

David said, "You come to me with sword and spear, but I come to you in the Name of the Lord of Hosts, the God of the Armies of Israel whom you have defied. Today I am going to cut off your head and give your flesh to the birds". Guess what? David did not have a sword, but he said, "I am going to cut off your head today". Goliath was furious, the Bible says Goliath moved towards David. David must have said, "offense? I am a master of offense". Goliath was still doing the giant march, but David ran quickly towards him. 1 Sam.17:48 (NLT) *"As Goliath moved closer to attack, David quickly ran out to meet him. 49 Reaching into his shepherd's bag and taking out a stone, he hurled it with his sling and hit the Philistine in the forehead. The stone sank in, and Goliath stumbled and fell face down on the ground."* Attack! Every time you attack, every time you move forward, heaven moves forward with you. Every time you take a step in God, heaven goes ahead of you. The Bible says that the stone David threw hit Goliath's head and sunk in. Then Goliath fell forward. If it was indeed the stone that actually killed Goliath; the stone traveling at a high velocity, hits Goliath's forehead, he should typically have staggered and fallen backwards right? But the Bible states clearly that the stone hit Goliath's head, he staggered and fell forward. That tells me that there was an unseen force just waiting for David to release his stone. As soon as David released the stone, it was guided to Goliath's forehead so that it would not look like nothing happened. As the stone touched Goliath's head, heaven whacked him on the head from behind and he fell forward. Read the Bible, Goliath fell forward.

ALWAYS AUDACITY!

~Courage Is Always Expressed In The Willingness To Go Forward~

Every time you take a step in God, heaven goes ahead of you. Note also that David saw Goliath and moved into action immediately. He did not first excuse himself to go and pray. David said this Philistine is coming down. God wants you to get up and attack. For some the attacking you need to do is in the area of education, you need to engage in some personal development attacking. Just get up and do it.

1Sam.30:8 (NKJV) "...and the Lord answered him, Pursue: for you will surely overtake them, and without fail recover all." You do not recover all on the defensive. You only recover on the offensive. For the principle of the offensive to work, it must be ignited with audacity – the willingness to take bold risks. You cannot be on the offensive if you are not courageous. You need courage. Fredrick the Great puts it this way, "L'audace, l'audace, et toujours l'audace." This translated in English means, "Audacity, audacity, and always audacity." I would urge you to write this down and put it before you at all times. For at least a month, let it be the first things you see in the morning and the last thing you see before you go to sleep at night. Audacity, audacity, and always audacity. Courage is always expressed in the willingness to go forward. God wants you to move forward and attack because you have been going around this "mountain" for too long.

The military will tell you that the most essential quality of a General will always be courage. A General must be an Intellectual, a Visionary, a Team Builder...etc... but these are not the most essential qualities. The most essential quality of a General will always be Courage. You are the general of your life. You need to have courage. You must have active courage. For instance, I have a spiritual son and one day he calls me up and was lamenting. There was this girl he wanted to marry, and the girl really liked him. But every time he went to see her, all they do is play Ludo [board games]. They had a good relationship and the girl was actually waiting for him to pop the question. While the waiting continued, some other man that the girl also liked, but not as much as she liked my son, came attacked, pestered her, bought her roses, and took her out. She was reluctant initially hoping for my son but the other man bamboozled her with love. Eventually she chose to go with the other man because she could not keep waiting and hoping my son will pop the question or at least make his intentions known. So, she got committed to the other man and then my son called me and was asking what he should do. I was angry, I said, "Who is your father? You cannot woo a lady?" He said that when he gets in front of her, he gets tongue tied. My friend, open your mouth and ask her out. "Audacity, audacity, and always audacity".

We have dealt extensively with active courage but there is a part of courage I came across in the one of books on war generals. Every war general must have Moral Courage. Moral courage is the ability to control yourself. The ability to say 'No!' to excesses. The ability to walk away from things that are enticing. As the general of your life, you need moral courage, it will save your life. Prov.25:28 (NLT) "A person without self-control is like a city with broken-down walls." What it means for a city to have broken down walls is that anyone can attack that city. You have to have the courage to say 'No' to pornography and to anything that will defile you. You have to have the courage to say 'No' to stealing and to lying. The beautiful thing about courage is, courage can be developed. You develop courage by acting courageous. Even though you are afraid, you shake off the fear and act as though you are courageous. Everyone that appears courageous knows fear. The more you act courageous, the more courageous you become. Ralph Waldo Emerson says, "Make a habit throughout your life of doing the things you fear; if you do the things you fear, the death of fear is certain". If you find that you lack the courage to woo a lady, go ahead and do it inspite of the fear you feel. When you do it, you will have confidence. If you find that in your business, you are afraid of knocking on doors. God says knock on it, so go ahead and knock on it. Someone said, "a hero is merely a coward who is brave five minutes longer". This is so true. In the first church I pastored, we came to a point we where going to acquire a land. The land at the time cost one hundred and sixty million. So, we had a meeting with the family and the head of the family was also in attendance. They asked us what we had to offer because there were other people also bidding for the same piece of land, a corner piece, the prime place. I told them we were going to make a down payment of five million and that we are going to start having services there in two weeks. A Pastor from another church was our church lawyer at the time. He would later tell me that when he heard my offer, he thought it was a lost cause. However, I thank God for him, and people like him. Like the Jonathan's armor bearer said to him, whatever is in your heart do it, I am with you. If you want to fall on the Philistines, I am with you [1 Sam.14:1-7, NLT]. The other Pastor (our lawyer) said he held himself back from challenging my position or suggesting a different position to me. The meeting got heated, the people felt insulted and were visibly upset. Some of them wanted to walk out of the meeting. I was afraid, but I maintained my position and was praying in tongues under my breadth. They put off an offer and suggested I take some more time to source for the funds. I said, "No deal! Five million and we are having services there in two weeks." The meeting was about to go south, I was about to cave in, I was just holding on to the God of heaven and waiting for Him to make a way. The all of a sudden, the head of the family spoke up and told everybody to keep quiet. The Yoruba culture is very heavy on hierarchy. She asked, 'Pastor what did you say?' I swallowed air; what did I say? Do I even have the courage to say it again? But I spoke up, "We will pay five million and we will begin to have services there in two weeks!" She looked at everyone in the room and her next words blew me away. She said, "What the Pastor has said is what is going to happen, take the money he is offering." Our lawyer confessed that he had never witnessed anything like that before in his entire life and the experience changed his life forever. I can confidently say that the hero is merely a coward that held on five minutes longer!

Courage is a habit, and you can develop it. The only person who has never fallen is the person who has never walked. Do not be afraid of falling. Big deal if you try and it does not work. Big deal! Get up and try again. Fear is actually based on exaggeration. Faith is based on inspiration. Inspiration is like exaggeration, it's God's Word that has exploded in your mind. You need to be courageous in the positive direction. Everybody that is fearful is courageous in the negative direction, they just don't know it. They are courageous. There is no dishonor in falling so why are you afraid to fall? The only dishonor is in failing to get up again. You failed your examinations so what? Take the examination again and excel at it. I see you breaking every curse in your life courageously. I see you walking into your destiny courageously in the Mighty Name of Jesus.

THE CORRIDOR PRINCIPLE

~The Only Person That Has Never Fallen Is The Person That Has Never Walked~

I will illustrate the corridor principle with the findings from a research that was done on a series of MBA graduates. The research showed that the people spend "X" amount of money and "Y" amount of time to get an MBA degree. Yet only 10% percent of the people that graduate from this Masters program go out to start a business and are successful. Whereas 100% of the class got the same teaching, the same tools but only 10% actually step out. The research was enormous, but the conclusion was the same; the people that did not step out did not step out because of the fear of failure. Of the people that stepped out, not one of them was even sure but they took the chance and became successful. They discovered that the people that did not do anything with the MBA coasted their excuses with big words. This quote by Andy Stanley sums it up perfectly, he says, "Fear often disguises itself behind the mask of care. Fearful people often excuse their fear as caution." Have you heard people insisting on being cautious and taking calculated risks? There is nothing wrong with taking calculated risks. However, when you don't take action after the "calculated risks analysis", you are just coating your fear with big words.

Here is the corridor principle; 100% of the people that stepped out and became successful, all of them said, the amazing success they encountered was not in the direction they initially set out to go. Success they say, almost always comes from a different place than anticipated. The key is commitment to take action. Stepping out is actually like stepping into a corridor, you think you are headed in a certain direction, but you come against a road block. Things happen and while you are trying to solve the problem, a door opens to your left. You take that door and you encounter huge success. This has also been true about my experience. When I resigned from paid employment, what I ended up doing was far from what I set out to do. But if I had not stepped out, I would not have discovered what I eventually began to do.

In modern warfare, there is a weapon known as the guided missile. The guided missile can be guided internally or externally. Ideally when a missile is guided, it is internally programmed. When it is lunched, it already has its target programmed into it. It may go around a hill, go down to sea level to avoid the radar and then go high up to avoid obstacles until it hits the target. The missiles are guided from a control center. A business book I read stated that after you have taken your step, you must believe that the 'universe' will make it happen for you. Universe? When I read it, I laughed because in my estimation, the authors really don't know God. What they are saying in essence is this, they do not know what it is but for everyone that steps out something guides them until they hit that target. As a child of God, you have been programmed as a missile for your destiny. You are going to dodge every enemy curse, rise above every enemy obstacle, until you hit your target you will not stop in Jesus Name. You are a missile, launch, believe that God will guide, that God will orchestrate, that the target will not be missed. Attack! Be on the offensive! Exploit, grab and seize for God is with you.

The Principle of the Offensive is, **"Advance and attack the opposition. Grab and exploit the opportunities."** As you journeyed through this chapter with God, I believe that the Holy Spirit drew your attention to certain areas where you need to begin to move on the offensive. You need to list out the areas and take immediate action.

CHAPTER 3
THE PRINCIPLE OF MASS

The Principle of **Mass**: "Concentrate combat power at the decisive place and time."

~Concentration, Focus Inevitably Creates Blindness And That Is Okay~

It would interest you to know that most war generals, regardless of their faith, have a copy of the Bible and they read it. Why is this so important? It is because all of these proven principles of war have their roots in scripture. Life is a battle. Right from when a child is born, the child experiences his or her first struggle in exiting the womb. Based on the world's expectations that a baby should cry when it first comes into the world, if that child falls short or does not cry, he can expect a whacking from the midwife. This battle, this struggle never really stops until he or she exits this world. Life is a battle and you are the general of your life. Remember David and Goliath? David took responsibility by challenging the Philistine hero Goliath, after all who is he to defy the armies of the Living God? God is waiting for you and me to take responsibility for spheres of influence.

2 Samuel 23:15 (NLT) "David remarked longingly to his men, "Oh, how I would love some of that good water from the well by the gate in Bethlehem." 16 So the Three broke through the Philistine lines, drew

some water from the well by the gate in Bethlehem, and brought it back to David…" The Principle of Mass is, Concentrate Combat Power At The Decisive Place And Time. In your business, there is a decisive place and time. In your family, there is a decisive place and time. The decisive place and time moves but once you discern it, concentrate combat power. Do not diffuse your energy, focus, concentrate. The three Principles we have discussed are linked (all the Principles are). Once you resolved to fight a battle, define *The Objective*. It is not every battle you should fight. Some battles you ignore. But once you have an objective, launch your attack. *The Principle of The Offensive.* Go on the Offensive. Do not just sit down and procrastinate. Launch your attack. How much time has passed between when you identified the objective and now? What are you waiting for? Be careful not to launch your attack in different directions. Concentrate your forces! *The Principle of Mass.*

In 1879 in the Southern part of Africa, the British forces had thousands of men fully equipped, carrying their banners and marching around intimidating the Zulus, the locals. But the Zulu chief was a very intelligent and courageous war General. He did nothing but send spies to watch the British forces. After a lot of military display, the British forces dispersed on an open field to relax. As soon as the Zulu chief got word that the British forces dispersed and were relaxing, he launched what is known as a buffalo head attack [it is a buffalo head formation]. He had fewer men, but he wiped out the British forces. In fact, that is the biggest loss that the British conceded to a local force in all the territories they took. Why was this possible? Simply because a man with fewer number of soldiers that were only armed with a shield and a spear concentrated his forces, attacked and conquered thousands of soldiers with more sophisticated weapons. Every great General understands the power in concentration of forces. You are the general of your life. So, how does this apply to your life? The Principle of Mass is, *concentrate combat power at the decisive place and time.* The key word there is concentrate and the opposite of concentration is distraction. What are the things that are distracting your forces? What are the things that are distracting you? Get rid of them fast! If you do not get rid of them, they will spread you too thin. You are going to dissipate your energy and you will be totally ineffective. As a business person and a leader, there are many things that I can do but I have chosen deliberately to focus and concentrate my forces on the things that only I can do. There are many things that you can do, particularly if you are one of those people with multiple gifts. But there are also things that only you should do. Focus your energy, concentrate your powers, get rid of distractions. Focus on the things that only you can do because that is what you should be doing. Delegation is the mark of great leadership. Identify people on your team that can do the other things that need to be done and let them do it.

In Luke 9:61 [NLT], this man asked to be Jesus' disciple, he probably realized that, judging by the way Jesus lived his life, he would not see his family in a long while. So, he asked Jesus for permission to go and kiss his family goodbye. If someone decides to devout his entire life to God, going to kiss his family goodbye is not such a bad thing, right? This shows us clearly that distractions are not necessarily bad things. In fact, a lot of the time, distractions are good things, but they are distractions nonetheless. Jesus' response to him shows what our attitude to distractions should be. In His response to the man, Jesus said something really profound. Luke 9:62 [NIV] "But Jesus told him, 'Anyone who puts a hand to the plow and then looks back is not fit for the Kingdom of God.'" [with emphasis]. When I first read this scripture, I struggled with it because I thought Jesus was being too hard on the man. Don't you think that response seems rather harsh? This man just wants to go and kiss his family goodbye! But Jesus says, "Anyone who puts a hand to the plow and then looks back is not fit for the Kingdom of God." The question is, why would Jesus respond this way to such a seemingly harmless request, considering that the man just signed up for discipleship? Why would Jesus call him "unfit" for the Kingdom of God? Jesus did not say, he that lays his hands on the plough and abandons the plough. This means the persons hands are still on the plough. Meaning his or her decision to follow Jesus is unshaken but the person has become distracted and looked back. Jesus says such a person is not fit because when ploughing, your focus should be on what you are ploughing. If you look away, your plough will shift off course attempting to follow your focus. That is how serious distraction can get and there is only one thing to do with distractions, eradicate it. Be brutal.

THE CITADEL STRATEGY

~ *You Cannot Be Effective If You Are Not Blind To Certain Things *~

The principle of mass is one of those principles that is effective both on the offense and the defense. A classic example of this in warfare is called the Citadel Strategy. In the days when cities and countries used to be physically walled, the strategy is to wall the outer perimeter of the city and then go further into the city and create another wall forming a concentric circle. Such cities would have sometimes three or sometimes five concentric circles of walls outside and within the city. During a battle, if the enemy breaks through the first wall, the forces will withdraw into the inner wall and keep withdrawing until all the forces are concentrated in a place called the citadel. Usually the family of the king would be in the citadel.

A citadel is a reinforced place, the last line of defense. The cities that have citadels hardly ever fall, because of the concentrated force in there they are able to hold off any kind of attack until an ally comes to rescue them.

How does the citadel strategy apply to you and I? The question is, if you were to lose everything, what is the one thing you must not lose, and from that one thing you can rebuild or regain every other thing you have lost? Think about it, I mean take time out to sit and ponder over what your one thing is because that is your citadel. I discovered mine years ago and it has saved my life. I discovered mine as a Christian, as a business person, and as a husband. You need to discover what your citadel is in the different facets of your life. I will tell you what your citadel should be as a Christian because it is the same for all believers, that is if you are a Christian. If you were to be stripped of everything, the one thing you should never lose as a Christian [your citadel, your last line of defense], is your relationship with Jesus. You must guard it with your life. Personally, I have gone through a whole lot. In the past, I lost so many things yet because of that one thing, my citadel of power was protected, I was able to bounce back and do better. If your employment is terminated, child of God, make sure you do not terminate your relationship with Jesus. If they strip you of your titles, child of God, make sure they do not strip you of your fellowship with Jesus. If you lose your physical possessions, child of God, please do not lose your ability to hear from God. As long as I can show up before God, connect with my Father, have fellowship with Him, and hear Him I am fine. I beseech you, no matter what life throws at you, do not turn your back on God. God is the surest thing in life. Even if you lose everything, as long as you continue to hear from God, you will regain everything. I know what my citadel is in my business, I know what it is in my marriage, and in the different facets of my life. You need to find yours out for yourself. What is your one thing?

A Italian economist came up with a theory called the Pareto Principle [also called the 80/20 rule or the 20/80 rule]. The Pareto principle states that, eighty percent of all your result is as a result of twenty percent of all your activities. Meaning, only twenty percent of what you are doing right now is producing eighty percent or more of the result you are getting. No matter how wealthy you are, it is only twenty percent of what you are doing that is generating the wealth. What you need to do and should do is, identify that twenty percent by all means and protect it. That is your "Citadel". Sometimes, it is a lot less than twenty percent, find it and by all means concentrate all your forces there. There are so many things I can do as a business man and as a Pastor that I have chosen not to do because they are not my twenty percent. I found my twenty percent and I have resolved to stay focused on it. As discussed earlier in this book, the acronym for focus that I think is so apt is, "Follow One Course Until Success". How long do you want to continue starting one thing and stopping another, starting yet another thing and stopping yet another thing? People that behave like this are hardly ever really successful, hardly! Focus, just follow one course until success.

As a leader in whatever sphere, you need to identify your twenty percent. It would surprise you to know that eighty percent of the result you see in church is produced by twenty percent of the people you see. This is also true about a lot of thriving organizations. It is only twenty percent of its people that are making things happen. My question to you is, who are your twenty percent in ministry, in business, in your organization? Every leader must find his or her twenty percent and protect them. Guess what? Sometimes, they are a lot less than twenty percent. David got it right on so many levels – as a war General, as a leader, and as a worshipper. David had a large army but there were a certain group of thirty men called, "The Thirty" also nicknamed the "Gibborim" in the Hebrew text. They were also referred to as David's special forces. David could lose all his soldiers but not the thirty because with the thirty, he can take nations back. Amongst "The Thirty", David had "The Three" scripture refers to them as, "The Three Mighty Men". Who are "The Three"? The Three are known not by their titles but for the sacrifices they make. 2 Samuel 23:15 (NLT) "David remarked longingly to his men, "Oh, how I would love some of that good water from the well by the gate in Bethlehem." 16 So the Three broke through the Philistine lines, drew some water from the well by the gate in Bethlehem, and brought it back to David..." David just expressed his desire and the three broke through enemy camp to get it for him, remarkably sacrificial! It would be erroneous to tag this as favoritism. It is not favoritism, it is leadership. If you do not lead like that, you are going to have a lot of problems. Jesus led like that; Jesus had "The Seventy", then from the seventy Jesus had "The Twelve", then from the twelve Jesus had "The Three", and from the three Jesus had "The One".

What is that thing that only you can do or should do in your house? Make sure you are the only one doing it. Ladies, why should your house-help be the one serving your husband food? A popular saying states that the way to a man's heart is through his stomach. While this many not necessarily be true for all men but you must understand the reasoning behind that saying, which is, one thing leads to another. If your house-help is the one serving your husband food, soon enough she would be serving him something else. I know this is not popular, but somethings just have to be said. In fact, Christians very often behave like the ostrich that buries its head in the sand and thinks no one can see it. There are certain things that only you should do, identify them and ensure that you are the only one doing them. I understand that some women are career women and entrepreneurs and all that. But trust me, no one else should mind your business for you. Your husband is your business, mind him! The point is, you need to find your one thing and concentrate your powers. Even the Apostles, at a point in their ministry, got to these crossroads. They must have learnt from Jesus what I am sharing with you now. Acts 6:2-4. What they said in essence is, there are many things we can do in ministry such as serving food, taking care of widows, visiting prisons, etc. But we give you this charge, find people that are spirit controlled that will do it, so that we can concentrate on our one thing - the ministry of the Word and to prayer.

Concentration is the power of focusing all of one's attention. When you focus, inevitably, you create blindness and that is okay. A lot of people do not want any blindness. The truth is, you cannot be effective if you are not blind to certain things. When you focus on one thing, you are going to be blind to another thing. You need to be comfortable with that. You cannot be everything to everyone. Concentration is a habit that can be developed. Bruce Lee was my favourite actor growing up. The man is not only an actor, he is also a martial artist. Bruce Lee said, "I fear not the man who has practiced 1,000 different kicks once, I fear the man who has practiced 1 kick 1,000 times." The man may not know the dragon kick or the tiger kick but the one kick he knows, he has practiced it repeatedly and mastered it. That is a man to be dreaded. Now imagine if this man focuses on hitting that one kick at a lethal target, he is not worried about hitting your hands but is focused at hitting your heart. You should do everything humanly possible to avoid such a person. As they say, he that fights and runs away lives to fight another day; that is wisdom. The Principle of Mass is concentrate combat power at the decisive place and time.

The battle of Austerlitz, one of the pivotal battles in Europe, also one of the most important battles for the great General, Napoleon. Austria and Russia formed an alliance, a huge army while Napoleon had a little army. Napoleon's objective was clear; his objective was not to eliminate all the enemy forces; his objective was to control the mountain - the highest point on the battle field. Even though he was losing men alongside he kept going. He fought his way until he took over the highest point and from there he defeated the largest force in Europe - concentration of power. As Christians, the mountain you need to climb is the mountain of prayer. You need to position yourself on the mountain of prayer. If you position yourself on the altar of God, you will dictate things in life. You will say to this, "go!", and it will go. You will say that, "come!", and it will come. In your personal life, you must be deliberate about positioning yourself on the mountain of prayer and taking your place in the spirit realm. I will tell you a secret a lot of people do not know, the heavy lifting happens at the mountain top because of the positional advantage it affords. I want to challenge and encourage you as a Christian to have personal vigils. Devout focused time for vigils where you position yourself on God's altar. Identify that key result area and make it happen.

FORCE MULTIPLIER

~ *A united concentrated force is mostly unstoppable.* ~

Mass has two components: concentration and unity. Because of these two components, the principle of mass is a force multiplier. It enables smaller forces to conquer a much larger enemy. How many soldiers went to get water for David? There were just three of them and the Bible says they broke through the camp of the Philistines. The phrase, "Broke through", means they fought their way through. Three men went against the camp of the Philistines comprising of hundreds of thousands of soldiers. These three men stayed together, back to back and compact. They penetrated and got to the other side and fetched the water. I can see them putting the water bottle on one person's neck and they went back through the same route. Why were these three men able to do this? It is because they had concentration and unity. Have you ever been in a meeting that when the people on your side of the negotiation speak, you are wondering whose side they are on. I have. A house divided against itself will not stand. Unity is too powerful to toy with.

A united concentrated force is mostly unstoppable, and this is true even in an ignoble mission. An example from Scriptures is the tower of Babel [Gen.11:1,3-7, KJV]. Unity is so important [Ps.133:1-3, NIV]. The enemy knows this, and that is why his number one agenda for marriages is to turn the husband against his wife. The enemy knows that once the husband and wife backs are against each other, he can go to sleep because the marriage will self-destruct. David's men had unity. In the Kingdom of God there has to be unity, there are no lone rangers in the Kingdom of God. There has to be synergy, there has to be unity. How do you think you are going to win if you do not concentrate your powers and if you do not have unity? You must go back and sort out the unity issues. Then get your concentration in place and launch your concentrated forces. No force on earth will be able to withstand you.

So, what is holding you back? For some people God has given you an instruction, you have the objective, concentrate your forces and launch. What is holding you back? Most times, you have to just trust God and take the step. For some, the step you need to take is to walk on water, just take the step. Some need to bite the bullet...do it, make the move, take the dive.

The story is told of a man that was falling from a very high height in the pitch dark freezing night. While he was in free fall, he was struggling for his life and crying out to God for help. Then suddenly a branch appeared from nowhere and he grabbed it and held it tight. After a while, his tired hands were failing so he again cried out to God for help. God spoke to him and said, "Let go of the branch." He said, "Let go? Lord, you know what I have gone through to get to this point so how can you be telling me to let go of this branch?" I have invested so much to get to this point, I cannot just turn my back now, Lord. God said,

"Let go of the branch." He convinced himself that this is certainly not the voice of God; how can God be telling me to let go of my only hope. The man held on to the branch and froze to death. In the morning, the news reported the story of a man that died hanging, holding unto a branch few inches from ground level. He was almost there but he refused to let go. The only reason why people do that is because they do not know what God has planned for them. Are you going to let go? Are you going to die on that tree in the cold or are you going to let go and let God? The ball is in your court?

CHAPTER 4

THE PRINCIPLE OF MANEUVER

The Principle of **Maneuver**: "Place the enemy in a position of disadvantage through the flexible application of combat power."

~ They Key To Successful Maneuvers Is Flexibility ~

Jn.3:6 (NKJV) "That which is born of the flesh is flesh, and that which is born of the Spirit is spirit… 8 The wind blows where it wishes, and you hear the sound of it, but cannot tell where it comes from and where it goes. So is *everyone* who is born of the Spirit." [with emphasis]. The Spirit of God maneuvers. No human being can predict His operations, His movement. When you think you have figured Him out, He shows up in another way. God's Word says, "…So is everyone that is born of the Spirit." Your enemy should not be able to predict your next move. In fact, even your friends should be left wondering and guessing about what you are up to. Why? It is because you move with the flow of the Holy Spirit; "as I hear I do" [John 5:30, KJV]. The principle of maneuver as it regards warfare simply states, place the enemy in a position of disadvantage through the **flexible application of combat power**.

As a child of God and the general of your life, you have to consistently place the enemy in a position of disadvantage through your movements.

If the enemy had known that Jesus would resurrect on the third day, if the enemy had known that the Blood of Jesus will silence every accusation forever and give you and I undisputed victory, he would not have killed Jesus. (1 Corinthians 2:8, NLT) The Bible says, "…So is everyone that is born of the Spirit" and that includes you (if you are a child of God). It means when the enemy is expecting you to show up by the north gate, you show up from the east gate. When he is expecting you to draw out guns, you lift up high praises. When the enemy thinks all your cards are on the table, you bring out a joker. You are just on top of your game, unpredictable. I pray that you will be truly unpredictable and stay unpredictable because of your learning and application of the principle of maneuver in life's battle field.

FLEXIBILITY

~ There Is A Better Way Of Doing What You Are Doing - Be Flexible ~

Great military victories are entrenched in movements and maneuvers. The key to maneuvering successfully is flexibility. When you are dealing with God, don't be rigid, instead choose to be flexible and remain flexible. You cannot put God in a box, so you have to be flexible. Maneuvering is not possible without flexibility. God say sit down, or stand up, or speak, or keep quiet, or go, or stop. You have to be flexible to follow these maneuvers. You cannot insist on keeping quiet when God says speak because the previous instruction was keep quiet. It is "as I hear I do". I am a student of historical war. I have volumes and volumes of materials (books, CDs, DVDs, Magazines etc...) on historical campaigns and documentary videos of all the notable wars that have been fought in this century. These war generals were not necessarily Christians, but they used biblical principles to secure earthly victories. You would agree that there is much to learn from them.

George Washington was a master of maneuver. George Washington led the campaign for the war that broke the back of the British hold on America and his success came through deploying the principle of maneuver. He was trained in continental warfare and continental warfare has a lot to do with structure and order. Although George Washington had led a lot of battles, he had lost every battle up until the one where he deployed the principle of maneuver. He led the campaign against the British forces and he was losing because the British trained him. You cannot use the enemy's strategy against him and expect to win. So, right in the middle of battle George Washington changed his maneuvering. He invented the Guerilla Warfare. He said that the American spirit is an enterprising spirit. He did not have much success with training them in continental warfare tactics. Why? A lot of the soldiers were entrepreneurs, businessmen, farmers and he could not get them to do what the British had taught him to an elite level. So, what he came up with the "hit and run" technique. He will look for the weakest point in the enemy's array and strike at that point. Before the enemy, in this case the British, is able to gather, he will run and hide. He did this repeatedly until he depleted the armies of the British and the Americans gained their independence through maneuvering.

Your capacity to think even while you are in battle and maneuver will make a huge difference. Life does not play fair, things happen! Particularly things you do not bargain for. So, what are you going to do? It happens to everyone that is living under the sun, your case is not special – the same temptation. The question is, what are you going to do when you find yourself in that mix? The only answer is maneuver. That which is born of the Spirit is spirit and that which is born of the flesh is flesh. Your ability to continuously think outside of the box, innovate, and maneuver in the midst of battle is key for victory. Innovation is very crucial. Innovation simply means using what you have to achieve your desired result. Clear thinking is key to innovation. When you are able to think clearly and innovate, it results in excellence. Excellence inspires people and glorifies God. There is a difference between excellence and extravagance. People that lack innovation think they must be extravagant. But when you are innovative, you do not need to be extravagant. Excellence is simple. So be open to the Holy Spirit; do not be fixated on your way of doing things.

The story is told of a daughter who out of absolute love for her father, rearranged the entire living room just to suit her father. But when the man came home from work that day, his reaction to what she had done was the direct opposite of what she had imagined. Her father was really angry, "Who is responsible for this? Who moved my chair?" He went off on every single person in sight and one by one they quietly exited the living room, leaving just mother and father alone. After he had calmed down or, so she thought, the mother asked, "Have you even seen what your daughter did?" She apparently was wrong because she succeeded in setting off more reactions about his deep displeasure. "I want my chair where I want my chair!", he shouted. After everybody had gone to bed, the man eventually went and sat down where the daughter had put the chair. Then he realized that he had a better view of the television, which made the late-night show more enjoyable. The chair was even better positioned to catch the evening breeze. Now realizing his errors, the man felt rather foolish for reacting the way he had. The lesson is that there are better ways of doing what you are doing - be flexible! There are better ways of achieving the results you seek - be flexible!

What I am about to share next is a scene that God played out before me some time ago. In the scene, I saw someone standing beside a broken-down bridge. The person was obviously fixated on the broken bridge. The function of a bridge is access to places that otherwise would not be possible without the bridge, right? So, you can understand the persons fixation. Then God shows up and moves the person to the other side of the bridge, miraculous maneuver! I expected the person to rejoice and move on, keep making progress. But instead of rejoicing, the person went back to the bridge, lamenting and trying to fix the broken bridge. This scene is the story of some people's lives. God has given you an advantage, a miraculous maneuver and you are still lamenting about the broken bridge. Don't you know that if that bridge was important to your destiny, it would still be functioning? Since it is broken-down, it means that its time and usefulness has expired. The important thing for you is that the wind of God's Spirit is going to take you to the other side - be flexible! You must be open to the wind of the Holy Spirit. Everyone that walks with God must acknowledge that God has a mind of His own. God is not your errand boy, you cannot give Him instructions. If this is who you think God is, then you are going to have a lot of problems with Him. God is God all by Himself. He has a mind of His own and He does what pleases Him. However, if you are attentive and you are able to adapt, what He is doing will not catch you unawares. For the children of Israel for example, it was the pillar of fire at night and a pillar of cloud in the day time. When and where the pillar stopped, the entire nation of Israel stopped. Once the pillar of cloud or fire begins to move, the entire nation must move with the cloud. If anyone insists on finishing his meal first before moving, what do you think would happen? The pillar is moving, and you have to make a choice, you can keep eating and be left behind or you can choose to follow the cloud and make progress. I believe strongly in my spirit that The Cloud is moving in a lot of lives and God is saying move with The Cloud! Be flexible!

THE TWIST

~Inquire Of The Lord, Never Assume, That Is The Key To Successful Maneuvering~

David was a master at maneuvering. Please read the story in 1 Sam.23:1-13, NLT. David's heart was with his people, Israel and even though he was running from Saul, he could not just stand by and watch the Philistines besiege and attack God's people in Keilah. So, David proposed to his men that they go and help Keilah. The men protested, reminding David that they were not safe in Judah so how can he be proposing that they make themselves even more vulnerable and risk their lives by helping Keilah, a walled city. The Bible says, "David inquired of the Lord, should I go?" and God said, "go!". On this premise, David again proposed the move and his men yet again protested because it was a dangerous move. The Bible says, "David inquired of the Lord again and God said, "go!" again so David engaged and delivered the city from the Philistines. Saul, of course, got wind that David was in the walled city of Keilah and he came to attack David. David got intelligence that Saul was coming, if Saul had allegiance with the city, they would give him up but if not then he would be safe. But the Bible says, David inquired of the Lord, "Will these people betray me?" When I read this, my thoughts were, why would the people of Keilah betray David? Then I realized that sometimes we assume that because we have helped people, they will also help us. We assume that because we have been good to people, they will be good to us also. Do not destroy yourself because that is not always the case. Of a necessity, always inquire of the Lord because that is the key to maneuvering. David did not assume, he asked, "Lord, will these people give me up?" and God said, "they will give you up." At that point, the default reaction for a lot of people is to get angry with the people of Keilah. However, David shows us that that is not the right response. David did not waste his time on anger, he just packed his bags and left. There are relationships that you need to exit even right now because like Keilah they will sell you out. It is my prayer that God will not give you up to such people in Jesus Name.

There is a supernatural twist to every battle. Like David, you and I must be able to hear God and act immediately we hear His voice. Audacity, audacity again I say audacity. In every battle, there are "forces" that can either be for or against you. I pray that the "forces" will not be against you in Jesus Mighty Name. Many years ago, I had to represent the company I used to work for at the time in South Africa. I met with our partners in South Africa and we went through all the necessary preparations for the presentation. I was supposed to make the presentation and when I was about to go, one man on the technical team shook my hand and said, "May the forces be with you." Sometimes, we think we are the only ones that know God. I did not want to say amen because I was not sure which forces he was referring to. So, I asked around about him and I found out he was a Jew. Every Jew knows that, "the horse may prepare for battle, but safety is of the Lord!" You should do your homework, you should plan, you should pray, and you should read, but every Jew knows that there is an unseen force that can back you up and make your life beautiful. Or can resist you and make your life miserable. I pray that the forces of heaven will back you up, in Jesus Name. I once saw a video of a football match and just when the game had started, there was a heavy wind. It is not unusual for football matches to be played in the rain, so they continued with the game. Team A had the ball and were heading in the direction of Team B's goal post. Kicking the ball was a struggle as it was as though the player was playing against the wind. When he finally got hold of the ball and kicked it, the wind carried the ball away from Team B's post all the way across the field into Team A's own post. They scored against themselves. Just in case you are wondering if such goals will be allowed, yes, it will. In every sport, it is common knowledge that you are not just playing against people but against the weather conditions as well. Except the umpire cancels or stops the game, but once the game is on, it is on. Guess what? The game of life is on and as your enemy kicks the ball, I pray that the wind of heaven will carry the ball into their own post in Jesus Name.

In another historic war called the six-day war, Egypt mobilized the Arab nations and their singular objective was to wipe out the nation of Israel. Egypt and its allies ignored the international community, surrounded Israel and were going to launch an attack and wipe out the nation of Israel. Israel was small compared to the opposition, but when the president of Israel saw what the situation was, he attached them first and in six days the battle was over. Take note that this battle was not fought in the days of David, this war actually took place in 1967. In the documentaries about the six-day war, the Jewish soldiers said that they saw angelic beings, the forces fighting for them. When they launched one rocket, its impact backed by angelic beings was greatly multiplied. All the Arab nations were defeated, not in three years, not in six years, not in six months, but in six days. I do not know what you are going through, but I need you to know that the forces of Heaven will work on your favor regardless of the strength of the enemy forces marching against you. In six days, you will not even be able to find them anymore, in Jesus Name. So be open to the wind of the Holy Spirit, Jn.3:6 (NKJV) "That which is born of the flesh is flesh, and that which is born of the Spirit is spirit… 8 The wind blows where it wishes, and you hear the sound of it, but cannot tell where it comes from and where it goes. **So is everyone who is born of the Spirit.**" [with emphasis].

COVENANT MANEUVERS

~Some Maneuvers Have Generational Impact – Be Flexible~

There are some covenant maneuvers in the spirit that speak for generations to come. There are sacrifices you can make now... seeds that you can sow now, that will not only shape your life but the lives of your generations unborn. For some, the prosperity they are enjoying today is as a result of what their parents had done. This is why you hear people complain about other people, 'I pray far more than he does, how come he always seems to get his prayers answered?' they say. There are a lot of people that are angry with me because in their opinion, the results I am getting far outweigh what I am putting in. They say, 'who does he think he is? Have you seen him pray? He does not know how to pray." To such people my only response is, I may not know how to pray but my grandmother prayed for me. My mother is praying for me. I was a little troublesome growing up, so a lot of praying went into my foundations and heaped on my head. Those women worked the miraculous roots in my life and what you now see is the miraculous fruit. You can do likewise for your generations unborn.

When my wife and I first started pastoring, there was a facility we rented for the church building. The facility was managed by the daughter of the owner and she gave us a tough time. There were meetings that would push every single Christian muscle in you to the limits. So, one day I went before God and I said I was going to possess the property because I was really upset. Back in the day, I used to be very volatile, but I am a lot more chilled now. I began to engage in the spirit, and I locked down the property. When I got to a point, God said to me, "I will not give you this property." I said, "No Lord, wherever the soles of our feet shall tread upon we shall possess." But God said insisted, "I will not give you this property", I did not know why. When He saw that I was not going to take no for an answer, He said, "I will give you your own... another property and it is a bigger place." A bigger place? I accepted the bigger place and I backed down. God kept His promise and I give all the glory back to Him. Then one day the mother, the owner of the property came to see me. She was a very nice, godly elderly lady. On her way out of my office, she stopped, and she began to apologize for all the trouble her daughter had caused. She told me that she had covenanted the property to God, it was only to be used for God's purpose. That was when I understood why I could not take the property even though the daughter was misbehaving. God is a covenant keeping God, He keeps covenants from generation to generation. There are things you are doing now that you think have no impact. Do not worry; It is your children that will enjoy the fruit thereof. Today, I am thankful and blessing my grandmother and my mother. There are some maneuvers you make in the spirit that rings on generationally, so be flexible. There are some seeds you sow in the spirit that rings on generationally.

Be open; one of the keys to being open is you must admit that you can be wrong. Always be open to the possibility that you may be wrong. I thought I could take the property, but I was wrong. Always be open to the possibility that you may be wrong, it will save your life. It will save you from praying unnecessary prayers. Napoleon Bonaparte, a French general, made the mistake of not being open to the possibility of him being wrong. Napoleon was a master of offense, of military movements and maneuvers. But Napoleon was defeated in the battle of Waterloo. That is where the statement, "You will meet your Waterloo" came from. My wife and I visited Brussels in Belgium during our honeymoon. Permit me to just say, if you are married or about to get married, please go for your honeymoon. If you are married but never went on a honeymoon, it is not too late. So, there we were at Brussels and our tour guide took us to Waterloo, to the battlefield that Napoleon lost, to the building where he was. They even preserved the table where he wrote the last letter to his brother. But why did Napoleon lose that battle? Napoleon had dealt with the British forces, his men came to him and said, "our maneuverings has given us an advantage. Let us finish the British forces." But Napoleon said, "No, we will take them out in the morning." But that night at 6 p.m. on the 18th of June 1815 the British General the Duke of Wellington made a statement that is attributed to the preacher John Knox. John Knox used to say, "Give me England or I die!" A lot of those generals study great men of God and learn from them. The British general said, "Give me Blucher or give me night!" In other words, give me Blucher or I die. Prince Blucher was a Prussian general. What the Duke of Wellington was saying in essence was, if he did not get help, Napoleon was going to wipe him out. The Prussian kingdom is a German kingdom and they were just next door. So, by 6:30 p.m. the Prussians bombarded Napoleon and by 7 p.m. Napoleon's men were wiped out. Napoleon ran for his life and that was the end of Napoleon the great. He could maneuver, he could attack, he could do anything, but he did not. He did not leave room for the possibility that he could be wrong, and it cost him everything he had worked for.

What the principle of maneuver does is, it puts your opponent at a disadvantage and gives you an advantage. However, NEVER forget that **an advantage is not victory**. Like in the game of chess for example, taking the opponent's queen gives you an advantage. However, this move gives the player a false sense of being in charge. A lot people that take the opponents queen early usually lose. For the opponent, it translates to increased zeal to fight to win and as such the game can easily tilt in favour of the opponent. God is going to give you an advantage and you are going to ensure that you focus and get your victory in Jesus Name. Jehoash, the king of Israel, went to Elisha for help. Elisha said fire your arrow, he fired the arrow. Elisha said that is the arrow of the Lord's deliverance. Then Elisha said to Jehoash, strike! Jehoash must have been happy to have a spiritual advantage. He struck only three times then stopped and Elisha was really upset, "Why did you stop? Now you will not have complete victory because you stopped." I pray that you will not stop until you get your victory in Jesus Name. For some people the story of their lives is like a goal keeper that catches the ball, but the ball always falls down and enters the net. In the Name of Jesus Christ of Nazareth, there will be no abortions in your life. Everything you conceive, you will bring to fruition in Jesus Name. Isa. 66:9 (NKJV) "Shall I bring to the time of birth, and not cause delivery?" says the Lord. "Shall I who cause delivery shut up the womb?" says your God." It is not in God's nature to make you conceive or empower you to catch something and let it drop. So everyone that has been close to victory and before now it has been eluding you, beginning from today you will not only see it you will eat from it in Jesus Mighty Name.

Sometimes, when you maneuver wrongly, it will get you into trouble. Some other times, some maneuvers have been done on our behalf by our parents, wrong decisions, wrong movements that have put you in the predicament that you are in. While driving to work one day, God gave me this scripture. Isa. 40:2 "Speak tenderly to Jerusalem, and proclaim to her that her hard service has been completed, that her sin [and the sins of her parents] has been paid for, that she has received from the LORD's hand double for all her sins." (NIV, with emphasis). If you receive this, your hard service has been completed. "Speak tenderly to Jerusalem, and announce to her that her time of forced labor is over, her iniquity has been pardoned" (HCSB, with emphasis). "Speak tenderly to Jerusalem. Tell her that her sad days are gone and her sins are pardoned... "(NLT, with emphasis) "Speak tenderly to Jerusalem, and cry unto her, that her warfare is accomplished, that her iniquity is pardoned..." (KJV, with emphasis).

The story is told of two orphaned siblings, an older boy and his little sister. The young boy was saddled with the responsibility of taking care of his sister. So, he started work on a farm. The pay was so little, but it was much more for people that worked extra hours. So, he struggled to get into one of the extra hours slots, but he never did get it because the supervisor only gave it to his own "boys". After a while, the boy's younger sister took ill and was going to die if she did not get the much needed medical care and medicine. But the boy could not afford medical care or medicine on the pay he was getting. He was not going to watch his only surviving relative die, and in bid to get out of the situation, he got into a dangerous maneuver. One day after work on the farm, he looked left and then right and when he thought no one was watching, he stole one chicken. He wrapped up the chicken, tucked it into his jacket and left. The money he got from selling the chicken went into the medical care and medicine his sister needed. And sure enough, she was revived. The next day after work, the supervisor approached him and told him he was going to work extra hours that day. The boy of course was overjoyed but his joy was cut short as the supervisor announced, "You are going to do the work but I am going to collect the money!" "That is not fair", the boy said, "how about we share the money?" But the supervisor refused and insisted on taking everything. The boy said, "In that case, I am sorry, but I would have to turn down the offer to work for extra hours". Just as he was leaving, the supervisor said, "remember the chicken" and he froze in his tracks. He knew what that meant and immediately he became overwhelmed with emotions of shame, guilt, and fear. So, that was how he began to work for extra hours, days ran into weeks and the supervisor was collecting the pay. After a while, the boy could not take it anymore so he protested and the supervisor said, "remember the chicken!" Each time he gets restless and wants to break free, the supervisor will remind him about the chicken. Then one day, the boy realized that he could die under the weight of this burden if he did not do something about it. He showed up early at work the next day, went secretly to meet the owner of the farm, falling on his face begging for mercy. "I sinned against you, I stole your chicken, and I am sorry. I am willing to go to prison if that is the punishment you decide but I cannot go on like this. Please forgive me!" "Get up", the farm owner said to him, "Get up, I have forgiven you!" So, the boy thanked him and then the owner said, "I saw you when you were stealing the chicken." "You saw me?" the boy asked in amazement. The farm owner smiled and continued, "I saw when the supervisor was extorting you, but I was waiting to see when you would get tired of being under forced labour, under his yoke and break free. You can go back to work." By this time, the boy who was weeping uncontrollably said, "Thank you! Thank you for be so merciful even when I deserved to be punished!" Then he got up and returned to work. At the end of the day, as he was leaving, the supervisor stopped him and asked, "Where do you think you are going?" "I am going home", the boy responded. The supervisor said, "You would have to work extra hours today as usual. Remember the chicken?" The boy looked at him, smiled and said, "What about the chicken?" and walked away. What forced labor are you under? The time is over! What sad days are you experiencing? Those days are over! What hard service have you been enduring? The service is over! "Place the enemy in a position of disadvantage through the flexible application of combat power." Sometimes, the greatest blow you can deal the enemy is to show up before God and ask for mercy and show gratitude.

CHAPTER 5
THE PRINCIPLE OF INTELLIGENCE

The Principle of **Intelligence**: "Do everything possible to gather and accurately interpret information that will enable you gain advantage and defeat the enemy."

~ *There Is No Recovery Without Intelligence* ~

It appears that every war general we see from modern history was a student of the Bible regardless of their faith. You are the general of your life so, you need to also be a student of God's Word and you need to understand how to deploy proven military strategies for obtaining victory in every area of your life. God has given and will continue to give you victory. However, you have to be aware of the victory we have in Christ Jesus and cooperate with God.

Prov.24:5 (NLT) *"The wise are mightier than the strong, and those with knowledge grow stronger and stronger. 6 So don't go to war without wise guidance; victory depends on having many advisers."* ★

Victory depends on having quality intelligence! Your opposition may be strong, but in addition to your strength you must be wise because the wise is mightier than the strong. Goliath was strong, but David was wise. Wisdom will floor strength any day. God wants you to gather intelligence and show up on life's battle field prepared. In marriage, in business, in your personal life and even spiritually, do not go to war without gathering quality intelligence. Do not launch without seeking counsel, weighing the counsel, and gathering quality intelligence. The scripture tells us that victory depends on gathering quality intelligence. The Principle of Intelligence is, do everything possible to gather and accurately interpret information that will enable you gain advantage and defeat the enemy.

It is one thing to gather information, but it is another thing to accurately interpret it. So, knowledge alone is not enough, understanding is key to accurately interpreting information that will enable you gain advantage and defeat the enemy. There are three levels of intelligence, three levels on which you must have accurate knowledge and intelligence. Firstly, you must know yourself. Secondly, you must know your allies. Thirdly, this is usually what most people focus on when it comes to intelligence is, you must know your enemy.

When it comes to intelligence gathering, most people focus on the third level alone and completely ignore the first and the second. But all three are key to intelligence gathering. Sun Tzu, Ancient Chinese General, in his book Art of War says, "If you know the enemy and know yourself; in a hundred battles you will never be in peril." This statement is consistent with scripture and we will get into it as we go deeper in this chapter. I strongly recommend that you get Sun Tzu's Art of War. Sun Tzu also said, "When you are ignorant of the enemy but know yourself, your chances of winning or losing are equal." In other words, when you know yourself and you do not know the enemy you are gambling with your business, gambling with your life, gambling with your organization, just gambling! It is time to stop gambling! Sun Tzu also says, "If you are ignorant of your enemy and of yourself, you are certain in every battle to be in peril." I can relate with this from my own personal experiences, where I have struggled with different things, I could pin it to these three things. In pastoring and as a sportsman, I see this play out consistently.

KNOW YOUR ENEMY

~ *Always Assume The Enemy Is Intelligent And Competent* ~

Great military leaders are constantly gathering and analyzing information. How can you be running a business and you do not know the vital facts, statistics, and information about that business? Something is definitely wrong with that. If after five minutes of talking to someone in business and asking questions, he or she is unable to answer basic questions about the business, I know that business and the owner will be in trouble real soon. It is your duty to gather information because you are the general. Information gathering is so important, and we can see this even in the way God works with His people. God has said to Moses and to the people of Israel, "I will give you the land but first chose twelve spies and let them go and gather intelligence" [paraphrased]. Why do they need intelligence when God already told them He was giving the land to them? Think about it. The answer is this: God is a God of Principles. He was teaching them the Principles of War. Today, Israel has one of the best Intelligence in the world (if not the very best), the Mossad.

In 1941, the Germans had a device called the enigma machine. The enigma machine has an encrypting algorithm that ciphers information on one end. Even though the information is intercepted, or the radio waves are tapped nobody is able decipher that information until it gets to the other end that has another enigma machine which can decipher it. The Germans practically took control of Europe because of solid Intelligence and coded communication. They could pass information around and nobody will be able to decipher it. Britain almost fell but Britain was smart. Britain went after one enigma machine, secretly captured it, and used it to decode all the German intelligence. Britain overpowered the Germans just by deciphering what is going on and what their plans were. Many times, Jesus would be with people and Jesus will "decipher" what was in going on in their hearts. People will have a thought in their hearts and Jesus would challenge that thought even before they speak. Jesus had an "enigma machine" of the thoughts of men. God wants you and I to be able to decipher the plans of the enemy. He wants you and I to be able to spiritually decipher what the enemy is planning.

In World War II, in the battle of Midway, the Japanese under the admiral Yamamoto, pushed back the American submarines and all their artillery. But unknown to admiral Yamamoto, the Americans paid attention to just one thing - decoding the Japanese intelligence. As soon as they decoded it, they did not only wipe out all Japan's equipment, they killed their general. They were able to kill him because they knew where he was [his location], and that he was going for an inspection [his itinerary]. The Americans knew that admiral Yamamoto was going to fly, so they just waited for him to take off and they shot down his plane. How does this relate to you and me? There is information in the spirit realm, you have to tap into it. You are a prophet of your life, note that I am not saying prophet as in an office. You are a prophet of your life and you need to understand this, inside of you is the Spirit of God. Jesus says this same Spirit will guide you, the Holy Spirit will teach you. You will hear a voice behind you saying, this is the way walk in it. Job for instance was minding his own business but there were discussions going on in heaven about him and he was clueless. Assuming Job was able tap into heaven and understand what was going on, perhaps he would have responded better. Perhaps, just perhaps he would have pleaded his case with God.

The story is told of how in a church meeting, two witches at sitting in different locations in the church hall communicated and said, now is the time to strike. The pastor intercepted the communication, so he stopped the meeting and said, "I heard what you just said, come out now!" and they both came. You have to be able to intercept communications and intelligence is so key. Most times, when I meet people, as I shake them just for fun and relationship with the Holy Spirit, I am asking Him 'who is this person?'. But it became very useful for me. So, I ask, "Who is this person?", He tells me, and He is always accurate. That alone has saved me a lot of stress. Ask and God will tell you. Sometimes, just one piece of information is all that is needed.

In warfare, people fall largely because they are ignorant and arrogant. One key attitude you must develop is to respect your enemy. Never ever take the enemy for granted, never! When you give the enemy respect, you will not take anything for granted. When people are arrogant, and they look down on the enemy, it is usually the first step to their destruction. Remember the story of Ai (Joshua 7, NLT)? The children of Israel looked at Ai and concluded it was a small town, so they did not need to waste time fighting Ai with their entire army. So, they sent just a few men and they gallantly lost – arrogance! So many people have failed exams because of arrogance. A student tells himself that he was born with the knowhow of calculus therefore rates the calculus exam to be a push over for him and when the result is come in it was failure. There is only one word for that and it is arrogance. With soccer for example, I have seen quality players stand in front of a penalty shot and because of arrogance, they miss the penalty shot. I have seen families disintegrate because spouses, instead of one to take care of the other, arrogance is the order of the day. Never underestimate the enemy, never-ever-ever-ever! **Always assume the enemy is intelligent and competent.** If you are wrong, then your victory would be a landslide. But if you are right, then you would be ready. Always assume that the enemy is intelligent and competent. In business, always assume that the competitor is intelligent and competent. At your job, always assume that the person vying for that same position is intelligent and competent, do your homework!

As Christians, we have an arch enemy of our souls, satan. Never ever underestimate the devil. I know we are victorious in Christ and we are seated in high places far above principalities and powers. Yes, I know that before the throne of God above we have a strong and perfect plea, a great High Priest whose name is love, whoever lives and pleads for us - I know! But do not underestimate the devil, there is nothing the devil cannot try. Many of us know God but we do not really know God. Until we see God, either die or are transitioned via rapture. When we see how majestic God is, that is when we will really know who God is. God is fearful to be praised, He is awesome, God is terrible. Guess what? The devil was Lucifer, he knew God is the Man of war, the Most

High. But he still tried God, so who are you? Excuse me, who do you think you are? Never think that the devil is a fool, you can call him many things but do not ever call him a fool. The devil is defeated but he is not a fool. Know your enemy. If he can launch an attack on God, knowing fully well Who God is, don't underestimate the enemy.

PERCEPTIVE

~ Do Not Be Casual With People That Can Change Your Destiny ~

In warfare, perception is everything and this is a dimension of knowing your enemy that you must be aware of. You must have heard it said because it is common knowledge that, who you know is more important than what you know. However, there is something more important than who you know and that is, who knows you. There are some people you know but they do not know you. You may remember them from secondary school and attempt to try to remind them about how your paths crossed in time past, but they do not know you. Who you know is more important than what you know. Who knows you is more important than who you know. But what they think about you is more important than who knows you. The fact that somebody knows you is one thing but what they think about you will determine the value of that relationship. Having access to someone's office because you know them, and they know you is one thing. But as soon as you step out of the office, they hiss and say, "Useless person" because they know that you are unreliable. They know that you are a cheat. What people think about you is their perception about you. Guess what? Perception is everything in warfare. It is not enough to drop names of people you know and that know you. The question is what do those people think about you? What they think about you is the most important thing and many times they would not tell you. As a business person, the way your customers think about you when your business name is mentioned, influences their buying decision. When your business name is mentioned, what your customers think about you is everything because the customer's perception is the customer's reality. Whether they are right or wrong, whether it is the truth, or it is a lie, what they perceive is reality. So in intelligence gathering, particularly in espionage, modifying perception is totally key. One of the rules of military intelligence, especially in the area of espionage, is to influence and shape the perception to your advantage. Remember the war general Alexander the Great? He allows his spies to be captured. The captured spies of course never talk but after they have been tortured, they will give false information. When the enemy checks all the spies (kept at different locations), the information is the same. So, the enemy will think they have gathered intelligence on Alexander, not knowing they are playing into his hands.

Perception also influences you and not just the enemy. There is a fantastic story on espionage and perception in the Book of Numbers 13 and 14 [NLT, please read it]. God instructed Moses to choose twelve spies that will go and check out the land of Canaan. Ten out of the twelve spies returned with a report that negatively shaped the perception of the entire nation of Israel. Be careful of the people around you, people that come to you with negative things that attempt to mar your perception. Two of the spies tried to influence the people positively but the ten's negative influence stood strong. The ten spies said, we saw ourselves like grasshoppers – perception. They also said, that is how the people in the land saw us. How did they know that was how the Canaanites saw them? In the story of Gideon for example, God had already gone ahead of Gideon to show the enemy a vision of a loaf of bread crushing their tents. So, the enemy was already afraid of Gideon and the armies of Israel. The enemy already had a perception which was shaped by a dream one of them had. All of Israel adopted the negative report from the ten spies and their perception was that they were like grasshoppers. In Numbers 14, God said, "as you have said it in My ears so shall it be." Be careful what you say, particularly in God's presence. Be careful what you say about your life because God is always with you. Their perception shaped their reality. That entire generation died in the wilderness.

Remember Genghis Khan of the Mongol empire? He was obsessed with possessing land and expanding his territory. The Khwarazm's empire was really large, and no nation had been able to dispossess this empire because they had a fantastic formation of defense. However, the northern part was left open because the northern part has a huge expanse of desert land and no army had been able to survive the desert. So, they just left the northern part open and focused on securing the east, west, and south. As you can imagine, that northern access was where Genghis Kahn went. However, he did not attempt to take on the desert like other forces had done preciously, otherwise him and his army would have died in the desert. Genghis Kahn captured a local village, the people that live in the dessert. But instead of killing them, he made them happy and gave them provisions. Overwhelmed by this good will, the people of course sought ways to repay and Kahn asked them for help with crossing the desert. The locals are the ones that know where the oasis are in the desert so, they led Kahn and his army from one oasis to another across the desert. By the time Kahn and his armies hit the Khwarazm's empire it was totally unexpected – intelligence. Kahn took time to gather intelligence and that gave him the advantage. There is no terrain that is too tough, the only reason why it appears tough is because you do not have enough intelligence. Remember the story of the little Egyptian boy in 1 Samuel 30? The Amalekites had burned everything and taken the wives and children of David and his men. David asked God, "shall I pursue, will I overtake, will I recover?" And God said, "pursue you will surely overtake and without fail you will recover all!" That was God's Word to David but on the way, David saw a little Egyptian boy who had been left for dead. David could have ignored that Egyptian boy because he already had a Word from God. But David knew that the fact that God has spoken to you does not mean you do not need intelligence. So, David fed and took care of the boy. "Who are you?" David asked, and the boy told him he was a slave of one of the Amalekite raiders. His master had left him to die. David asked the boy where the people were headed, and the boy gave David their entire military plan. David used that intelligence to recover all. There is no recovery without intelligence. God has said you will recover, but you need to gather intelligence.

There is someone you know that knows what you need to get to your next level. Who is that person? Who is that person that you can easily despise? The intelligence for your total recovery may just be with him or her, that is how God works. In your finances, in your spiritual life, in your business, and in your home, for that next level that you desire and envision, there is someone you already know that has the intelligence that will get you there. You may even be sitting beside the person right now. Many people have treated the person that holds the key to their next-level shabbily because they are not discerning. The people you think have nothing to offer you are actually the people who deserve the best treatment from you. Like that Egyptian boy, a lot of them have the information you need for victory. You have to treat everybody nicely because you just never know. It is not enough to know that there are people around you that may have the intelligence that you need, and it is not enough to treat people nicely, you have to ask the right questions. You are sitting beside someone that has gone a thousand kilometers ahead of you, spiritually for example, if you do not ask the right question, you will leave that meeting without getting anything. Asking the right questions requires that you think and think clearly. I remember sitting down with Craig Groeschel, the Pastor of Life Church. I recognized my hunger for knowledge and I also recognized that Craig knows more than I do. I cannot pretend, and arrogance will not take anyone anywhere. So, I channeled all my hunger into quizzing him. The truth is you cannot begin to ask questions until you know that you do not know. Beyond the answers he gave me, I was keenly interested in how he thinks. Understanding how leaders (generals) think is so powerful.

On the subject of asking the right questions, some people will come to you with "questions", but they are not really asking questions. They already know what they think is the answer to the question because they just want to impress you with the answers, they think they know. When such people come to me, I delay in answering their "questions". They will quickly jump in and tell you the answer. My response usually is, "That is one way of looking at it", and they will go because they have fulfilled their objective. There are people around you that have what can change your life, you need to squeeze it out. Take the woman with the issue of blood for example. On the day she got her healing, there was a crowd of people around Jesus, pushing, touching and rubbing shoulders with Him. But that woman said, "If I can touch them hem of His garment, I will be made whole." She touched the hem of His garment and she was made whole and immediately Jesus said, "Somebody touched me." Peter could not understand it, how can Jesus be in a crowd and yet complain that someone touched Him, people had been touching Him all along. But Jesus insisted, someone touched me, the woman owned up, and you know the rest of the story. What I am pointing out to you is this, **do not be casual with people that can change your destiny**.

I told you the story of how the U.S. broke the code of Japan during World War II. The U.S. also knew that the Japanese are very intelligent, and they have brilliant programmers that could decode anything. If they were to come up with a code, it would just be a matter of time before the Japanese would break it. Guess what the U.S. did? I call it information maneuvering. They discovered a local tribe in Arizona called Navajo tribe. These tribe speak a language that is not documented, only a few thousand people speak it, and this local Indian tribe is resident in Arizona. The U.S. simply carried hundreds of Navajo natives, distributed them on their warships on their different bases, and they spoke Navajo across open communication lines. The Japanese picked up their communication, ran it through all their programs and nothing came up. So, because of that small Navajo tribe, the U.S. won the second World War, they devastated Japan. Think about it, the Navajo tribe was already in the U.S. all along. The people that will determine the victory were already there. There are people in your life that would determine your victory and they are already there in your life. It is your job to find them out. The Navajo tribe, like the Egyptian boy, could easily have been ignored. They were just an Indian tribe, a residue of the natives. But the U.S. understood that codes are just a language that cannot be understood by just anyone. So, why spend money on building ciphers when you have people that can speak a language that nobody could understand.

In 2 Kings 6:8-23, the Bible tells us of how the king of Aram would plot a military campaign to attack the king of Israel and Elisha would hear what they are saying in his own house and would warn the kind of Israel. It is so beautiful to be in your house and hear what people are saying in their own houses. This happens to me, most times unsolicited, I hear conversations people are having in their houses. So, the king of Aram after many unsuccessful attempts at his military campaigns, called a meeting with his generals. I can imagine him pulling out his gun and firing two into the air, putting the smoking gun on the table and saying, "who amongst us is betraying us?" The generals respond, "It is none of us but there is a prophet in Israel that hears the things you say in your bedroom." May your walk with God be that intimate, that when people are saying things about you, you will hear it because God wants to preserve you. If you were the king of Aram what would you do? I probably would try to be Elisha's friend. But guess what the king of Aram did? He sent his soldiers to go and arrest Elisha, an army versus one man. They arrived at Elisha's house and surrounded it. When Elisha's servant got up in the morning to fetch water, he saw them and ran back to his master crying, 'Alas my master, we are in trouble, they have surrounded us.' Elisha probably said, 'is that why you have woken me up? Relax there are more with us than are against us. I have intelligence, I can see chariots of fire. Can't you see the chariots of fire, boy?' His servant must have replied, 'I cannot see what you see sir, all I see are the enemy forces!' Elisha says, 'Alright, close your eyes, now see.' As soon as the boy could see the chariots of fire what do you think happened to his fear? It was replaced with confidence and both of them marched out. Elisha asked the Lord to smite the army with blindness. Note that it was not physical blindness. Then Elisha walked up to them and ask who they were looking for. 'We have come to arrest prophet Elisha!' they said. Elisha said, 'Is that the person you want to arrest? Come, let me take you to where he is.' So, Elisha led them into the middle of Israel and then prayed that God will open their eyes. When the eyes of their understanding were opened, they realized where they were and saw that they were surrounded. The king of Israel said to Elisha, 'Should I kill them?' 'How can you kill the people God has delivered into your hands?' Elisha said, 'feed them and send them back' [paraphrased]. The king of Israel did as Elisha advised, fed them and sent them back. The Bible tells us that from that day forward, the king of Aram did not trouble Israel. I pray that because of the superiority of your intelligence, everything representing the king of Aram in your life will hear your name and back down.

KNOW YOUR ALLIES

~ Greater Than The Enemy Without Is The Enemy Within ~

Who are the people around you? Do you know the people around you? Who are your allies, the people that appear to be on your side, who are they? Do you know them? I would advise you list the people around you and take their names to God and find out who they are. Some people have been married for twenty years but they do not know their spouse. While you are sleeping at night, your spouse morphs into an air vice marshal but you are totally un aware of who you are married to. You need to know everyone that is around you and what they are capable of doing. As a leader, if you do not know what everyone around you is capable of doing, you would be in for surprises. Sometimes, the Bible tells us that Jesus deliberately did things to test His disciples. To see who will say what and who will respond how. Sometimes, that is the easiest way to know. But at other times, you may need to wait and watch. Sometimes, God will reveal it to you directly, but you must know everyone around you. Who is capable of making certain decisions? Which of your children is capable of knowing that this is mommy's food or daddy's food and still eating it? If you do not know, try it, do it deliberately. There is probably one of your children that will eat it know it is your food because he or she wants to see that you would do. Do not break his or her head, just know and update your database. Just know who is capable of doing what. Do you know how Julius Caesar died? Have you ever heard the statement, "et tu brute" ("and you too Brutus")? Julius Caesar, a Roman Emperor, was daggered to death by Brutus his friend. When Brutus plunged the dagger into him, he could not believe it. He knew he had enemies but, "et tu Brute? (and you too

Brutus?). I pray, in the Name of Jesus Christ of Nazareth, that your last words will not be "et tu Brute"! My grandmother would say in Yoruba, "Bi iku ile oba pa ni, t'ode ole pani!" Meaning, if you are not destroyed by the internal enemy, the external enemy cannot destroy you. It is good to know the enemy without but your greatest risk, greater than the enemy without is the enemy within. There are people that if you fall, they just want to be in that position of saying, "Oh sorry, let me help you up!" Such people are dangerous. There are some people that are praying that you that you fall so that they can say, "We are all human after all, we forgive you." Check the people around you. In fact, you have to constantly check because people change, some people get better and some get worse. There are different versions of the story of Lagos, but I will tell you the story that one of the Idejo's told me. This is the story of Lagos; the oba [the king] of Lagos had always been prosperous. He had many wives, but he had one special wife. The oba of Benin, in expanding the Benin kingdom had launched several campaigns against the oba of Lagos but failed. The oba of Lagos had always been able to defend his territory. But the king offended his special bride. So, the special bride went and married the oba of Benin with intelligence and revealed his secrets. As you can imagine, the next campaign of the oba of Benin was a wash out. Who in your life is that queen? But the oba of Lagos was very wise, he immediately divided his land and gave it to his children [they are called the Idejo's] and conceded to the son of the oba of Benin, Ado. Till this day, the oba of Lagos is determined by the oba of Benin. But the oba of Lagos, coming from Benin, do not own a single plot of land in Lagos – not one. The Idejo's own the land – strategic thinking! So, you have the Olotto of Otto, the Onikoyi of Ikoyi, the Oniru of Iru, and the Oluwa's of Apapa. But why did Lagos fall that till this day the oba of Lagos is determined by the Oba of Benin? It is because there was somebody within that betrayed the king. I have news for you not everyone around you is for you. I am not saying you should go around and suspecting everybody. It is just a fact. As believers, we depend on the Holy Spirit for intelligence.

KNOW YOUR ALLIES

~ Greater Than The Enemy Without Is The Enemy Within ~

Do you know the people around you? Who are your allies, the people that appear to be on your side, who are they? Do you know them? I would advise you list the people around you and take their names to God and find out who they are. Some people have been married for twenty years but they do not know their spouse. While you are sleeping at night, your spouse morphs into an air vice marshal but you are totally unaware of who you are married to. You need to know everyone that is around you and what they are capable of doing. As a leader, if you do not know what everyone around you is capable of doing, you would be in for surprises. Sometimes, the Bible tells us that Jesus deliberately did things to test His disciples. To see who will say what and who will respond how. Sometimes, that is the easiest way to know. But at other times, you may need to wait and watch. My grandmother used to say, "It takes 1 day to know a thief but it takes 7 days to know a witch". Sometimes, God will reveal it to you directly. You must know everyone around you. Who is capable of making decisions? Which of your children is capable of knowing that this is mommy's food or daddy's food and still eating it? If you do not know, try it, do it deliberately. There is probably one of your children that will eat it knowing it is your food because he or she wants to see that you would do. Do not break his or her head, just know and update your database. Know who is capable of doing what.

Do you know how Julius Caesar died? Have you ever heard the statement, "et tu brute" ("and you too Brutus")? Julius Caesar, a Roman Emperor, was daggered to death by Brutus his friend. When Brutus plunged the dagger into him, he could not believe it. He knew he had enemies but, "et tu Brute? (and you too Brutus?). I pray, in the Name of Jesus Christ of Nazareth, that your last words will not be "et tu Brute"! My grandmother would say in Yoruba, "Bi iku ile oba pa ni, t'ode ole pani!" Meaning, "if you are not destroyed by the internal enemy, the external enemy cannot destroy you". It is good to know the enemy without but there is a greater risk, greater than the enemy without: the enemy within. There are people that wants you to fall, because they want to be in a position of saying, "Oh sorry, let me help you up!" Such people are dangerous. They don't necessary want you destroyed, but they want you to be at their mercy. Check the people around you. In fact, you have to constantly check because people change, some people get better and some get worse.

There are different versions of the story of Lagos, but I will tell you the story that one of the Idejo's told me. This is the story of Lagos: the oba [the king] of Lagos had always been prosperous. He had many wives, but he had one special wife. The oba of Benin, in expanding the Benin kingdom had launched several campaigns against the oba of Lagos but failed. The oba of Lagos had always been able to defend his territory. But the king offended his special wife. So, the special wife went and married the oba of Benin with intelligence and revealed the secrets of the oba of Lagos. As you can imagine, the next campaign of the oba of Benin was a wash out. Who in your life is that queen? You need to answer that question. Back to the story: But the oba of Lagos was very wise, he immediately divided his land and gave it to his children [each child is called an Idejo] and conceded to the oba of Benin, Ado. Till this day, the oba of Lagos is determined by the oba of Benin. But the oba of Lagos, coming from Benin, do not own a single plot of land in Lagos - not one (except magnanimously given by one of the Idejos). The Idejos own the land - strategic thinking! So, you have the Olotto of Otto, the Onikoyi of Ikoyi, the Oniru of Iru, the Oluwa of Apapa, Elegushi, Olumegbon, Aromire, Onisowo, Onitolo, Ojoro...etc. But why did Lagos fall that till this day the oba of Lagos is determined by the oba of Benin? It is because there was somebody within that betrayed the king. I have news for you, not everyone around you is for you. I am not saying you should go around suspecting everybody. It is just a fact. As believers, we depend on the Holy Spirit for intelligence.

KNOW YOURSELF

~ *Unto Yourself Be True* ~

Greater than the enemy without is the enemy within but even greater than the enemy within is yourself. One of the greatest disservice you can do to yourself is to think you are who you are not. Some people pretend to be who they are not long enough that they begin to believe it themselves. That is one of the greatest disservice you can do to yourself. Unto yourself be true, to know yourself. There are three steps to knowing yourself. The first step to knowing yourself is, unto yourself be true. Be brutal about telling yourself the truth. The second step to knowing yourself is, look into God's Word. The Word of God is like a mirror, look into it and you will see. The third step is, ask the Holy Spirit and He will show you yourself. Once you know yourself, then you can grow. You must know first and foremost that, "I am a liar and I like lying". Then you can change and grow; you can read books that will help you stop lying, you can get help. Know yourself.

Society used to be divided between those who have more and those who have less. But going forward, society is going to be divided by those who know more and those who know less. Knowledge is going to be the key decider. Your life only gets better when you get better. You cannot get better if you do not even know where you stand. Everybody wants their life to get better but that cannot happen if individuals do not get better. So, the more you acquire and apply accurate information about yourself and achieve results, the more valuable you become and the better the quality of your life. The good news is, there is no limit to how much better you can become by continuous learning. It is totally up to you. So, read books. You cannot afford to say you do not like reading. I have not always liked reading either, but I force myself to read. Now it's a part of my life. Nobody likes hard work. I am certain if given the option that everyone would prefer to have ant sized work and elephant sized pay. You have to listen to messages. Do the work, improve yourself, become better. Take that course. Listen to that advice, it may be bitter in your mouth right now but listen to it. Keep getting better and your life will get better. The truth is, your life only gets better when you get better. If I am consistently giving someone advice or feedback and I notice over time that the person is not listening, I stop. It is not because I hate the person but because it is not adding any value. Until you get to that point yourself when you recognize the importance of listening to advice, you cannot get better.

Another thing you need to know is, no one is "better" than you. If anyone is better than you, they simply know something you do not know, and they are simply doing something you are not doing. So, what should you do? Go and find out, know what they know, and begin to do what they do. You will find out that you will become better yourself.

When we were growing up, if I got the ninth position in a class of twenty-five students, my mother would say to me, "The person that came first, does he or she have two heads?" It drilled into me that, no one is better than me - no one is better than you! You are as good as you want to be. Where you are today, is where you want to be. It is your choice; do you want to die there or will you become better? Are you going to bite the bullet, take the bitter pill and be the better person? Or are you going to blame it on how "hard" life is and how much there is to read. Some people have believed the lie that they cannot catch up, so there is no point trying. It is a lie, you can. There is no limit to what you can learn. There is no limit to how you can improve your life – there is no limit! You have to know yourself.

Spiritually you cannot grow if you do not know yourself. You cannot fulfill your destiny if you do not know yourself. In first five chapters of the book of Isaiah, prophet Isaiah had been saying to everyone, including king Hosiah, 'Woe are you for doing this, woe are you for doing that, ...' Isaiah was just cursing everybody. Then the Bible says, on the day king Hosiah died, Isaiah saw the Lord. When you are so critical of people, it is because you have not see the Lord. When you see the Lord, you will stop being critical of people. In Isaiah's case, the king [his main object of criticism] died. (Read Isaiah 6, NIV) Isaiah said, "I saw the Lord highly lifted up and His train, His robe filled the temple. And I saw the Seraphim shouting Holy! Holy! Holy is the Lord God Almighty. And the temple shook and there was smoke all over" [paraphrased]. Then Isaiah finally saw himself and he said, "Woe is me for I am undone!" When you see people that are critical of others, it is an indication that they do not know themselves. If you see people that are quick to judge other people, it is because they have no clue about who they are. If you really know who you are, it humbles you. Knowing who you are helps you acknowledge that God's grace is the only reason why you are standing. It is by God's amazing grace that I am who I am. Isaiah saw himself and realized that he was an ordinary man like everyone else, prone to errors. Before this, he could only see the people that were undone but after he saw himself, he saw himself as part of them. God touched Isaiah, cleansed him, and commissioned him. Note that Isaiah was a prophet before then but until he saw himself he could not enter into his destiny. Know yourself!

CHAPTER 6
THE PRINCIPLE OF SECURITY

The Principle of Security: Never permit the enemy to acquire an unexpected advantage. **Cover your bases**.

~ Excellent Leaders Practice "Crisis Anticipation" And "Scenario Planning" ~

1Pet.5:8 (NLT) "Stay alert! Watch out for your great enemy, the devil. He prowls around like a roaring lion, looking for someone to devour. 9 Stand firm against him, and be strong in your faith…".

God's instruction to you and I is, stay alert and stand firm! Every top military general focuses not only on success but on survival. Success is one thing, survival is another. Gaining grounds is one thing maintaining grounds is another. Once you have achieved an objective, you spend the rest of your energy defending the territory. Take your career for example, you have achieved the objective of getting a job, right? Guess what? There are other people that are hoping that you will not show up at work so that they can take that job. You have to maintain the territory you have gained. It could be marriage for instance; there are other men eyeing your wife, you need to protect your territory. There are little Mrs. Potiphars eyeing your man, so you need to protect your territory. Another example is weight loss or weight gain; you have achieved a milestone, you need to protect that territory otherwise you will lose it. For every ground you gain, in every area of your life, you need to protect it. The principle of security simply states; never permit the enemy to acquire an unexpected advantage, cover your bases.

Great military generals never ever allow themselves to get complacent. In 1579, the battle of Quebec in Canada, North America. The French had control of the fortress of Quebec and from the fortress they controlled the territory. In fact, they had enjoyed a hundred and fifty years of domination in that part of North America. But interestingly, the French did not cover their rear, they did not cover their bases. Behind the fort of Quebec was the mountain. The mountain was too steep and always too cold but particularly too steep for any army to climb. But there was an Indian native that went to the British and said to them, we know a path through that same steep mountain that can give you access to the fortress of Quebec. The British general marched every single man in his army up the path- all day-all week, until they quietly climbed the plain of Abraham and they set themselves in array. The French had no knowledge of it. In the morning, they struck the French from behind and in ten minutes the two French generals were killed, and the French army was in disarray. An advantage of a hundred and fifty years was lost in ten minutes all because they did not cover their bases. What are you taking for granted in your business? what are you taking for granted in your health? what are you taking for granted in your marriage? what are you taking for granted? Cover your bases, always protect your flanks.

To be successful in security you must understand that **victory and defeat are always possible**. However, there are people who think because they are Christians and are seated with Jesus in the heavenly places, defeat is not possible. In this life, on this earth, if you take things for granted defeat is possible. This is why you have this book in your hands. Pay attention and put into practice every single principle. Always remember that victory is possible and so is defeat. Bernard Baruch says, "When business is good, people believe that it will always be good. When business is poor, people believe that it will always be poor. Neither is correct." When business is good always remember that business can be poor, so plan for both good and bad. In other words, always plan for the best and plan for the worst. Most people plan for the best but would rather wish the worst away. A lot of people do not even want to consider it, as soon as the thought crosses their minds they reject it "in Jesus Name" very quickly. But that is not how God wants us to respond. God wants us to be pragmatic and think. While it is fantastic that things are going on well, but please plan for when things will not go as smoothly. If things are not going smoothly, relax, this season is going to expire. Plan for when things begin to change and go on well. The reason you and I must plan is this, many people are destroyed by sudden breakthroughs [sudden promotions] that they are not ready for. Because they are unprepared, they respond to the promotion wrongly. People experience breakthroughs and start behaving like rascals because they did not plan for the best. God wants us to plan for the best and plan for the worst.

3 Jn.1:2 (NLT) "Dear friend, I hope all is well with you and that you are as healthy in body as you are strong in spirit."

This scripture highlights three key areas where God wants us to do well in. Firstly, God wants you to prosper, you need to get that in your mind because sometimes that is the shift that needs to happen. A lot of people are not sure if God wants them to prosper. I know how that feels because I used to struggle with that feeling. I was not totally convinced, there was still something nagging in me that maybe God does not want me to prosper. Guess what I did? I put it to death mentally; I got all the books I could get, and I read all of them. I got all the messages I could get, I soaked them in until I stopped thinking like that. God wants you and I to prosper, you must embrace it. God wants you to be in health, to be healthy. God wants you to be spiritually sound and spiritually strong. You must embrace it.

However, there are three key questions that we must ask concerning these three key areas. A lot people shy away from these three key security questions. I can assure you that these three key security questions will make you uncomfortable but as you go through the process you actually become stronger:

#1. Examine your relationship, your health, your finances, your spiritual walk; what is the worst possible thing that could ever happen in each of these areas? Think about it! What is the worst possible thing that can ever happen in your finances, in your marriage, in your health, in your walk with God? Think about each area.

#2. What can be done to make sure it never happens? What pathway down that hill must your block, or station men, or sentries with guns so that peradventure someone shows up, he or she gets roasted?

#3. How do you respond, if haven done all it still happens?

Think about different areas of your life, go through each question and rehearse your response. I was listening to the late Dr. Miles Munroe and he asked a question that boggled my mind he said; what is that one thing that if it happens, it can throw your life off balance? He said for him it would be to lose his wife and his children. He said he knows that he may never recover if he loses his family, so he stepped back, and he has attended their funeral (in his mind). He said he played out all the emotions and he chose how he will respond. He decided that he will not curse God, he will still believe God. I was like this is too strong for me, at the time. But I did it. You have to think. That is why when things happen, people begin to curse God and do all sorts of strange things. Job's wife advised him to forget about his integrity, curse God and die. After all, this same God did not protect his children, did not prosper him, or make him healthy. What are you still doing going to church every Sunday? This Jesus that cannot give you a job or give you a spouse. Tell the devil to shut up!

One of the things that helps us to build resistance is, you have to be ready. Do not be caught napping. While there is no way that you can be 100% ready, but you must have done proper scenario planning. Think about it. For instance, I know that God wants me to prosper financially. So, what can possibly go wrong in my finances? The worst possible thing that could happen is bankruptcy, getting to zero and negative. I have thought about it and you should too. What can be done to make sure it never happens? I have thought about that as well and I have put systems in place to ensure that I never get to zero or borrow in my life. In fact, I did a whole teaching that can help you titled, "Thinking Clearly About Finances" and it is available on the GFH Thrive Podcast absolutely free. In the message, we highlighted five things that you need to do and if you do them, you will keep moving forward and you should never get to zero. Tithing for instance, God says, when you tithe, He would rebuke the devourers for your sake. God promises to take care of the things that can take you to zero. Saving for instance, it is only a foolish person that eats everything he or she earns. Where were you five years ago, where are you today? Saving is wise. Subscribe to the Thrive Podcast and download the message for free, it will help you.

If after you do the five things that were listed in that message, how do you respond if it still happens? I have an answer to that also, it is personal. If for some reason that ever happens to me, I have friends that will ensure that my family never suffers. I do, I have more than one, do you? Jesus said, make for yourself friends that will take you in when you have financial disaster. I have people that will make sure that my wife and children never suffer if something were to happen to me, or if I were to go financially broke. How do you find such people? Do you really want to know? I will tell you; you be such a person for some people. There are people today, that without even praying and fasting, that if something happens to them, they know that this man will not allow their family to suffer and they are correct. What you sow is what you reap, that is how life works. I have gone through all these for every area of my life. It is tough, but you have to do it. Take your health, ask the hard questions. Take your spiritual walk, ask the hard questions. The worst possible things that can happen to your spiritual walk is apostasy. What can you do to make sure you never backslide? I have thought about it and I have put things in place to ensure that I never backslide. What if after all, I still backslide? I have it in place, ready to be launched. I have people in my life that will set me straight if that happens. Do you have such people in your life? These hard questions guarantee your security. Life, they say, is not a bed of roses - ask Job.

Horatio G. Spafford was a successful lawyer and business man, he lived in Chicago with his family. He was a Presbyterian church elder and was tithing faithfully. He supported D.L. Moody's ministry and built orphanages. Horatio Spafford did so many good things. He was into real estate and during the great Chicago fire, he lost everything. In that same year, his only son died. Two years later, his wife and four daughters were traveling by boat to Europe on a vacation when suddenly the ship capsized and only his wife survived. That was when she sent him that famous telegraph, "Saved alone, all is lost, what shall I do?" He practically took the next ship to Europe, to go and console his wife. As they got to the spot in the sea where the other ship capsized, the sailor pointed it out to Horatio. He was passing over the grave of his four daughters. Imagine the agony that he felt but Horatio sat down, and he wrote;

It is well with my soul by Horatio Gates Spafford (1828 – 1888)

When peace, like a river, attendeth my way, When sorrows like sea billows roll: Whatever my lot, Thou hast taught me to know, It is well, it is well with my soul.

(Refrain): It is well, it is well, With my soul, with my soul, It is well, it is well with my soul.

Though Satan should buffet, though trials should come, Let this blest assurance control, That Christ hath regarded my helpless estate, And hath shed His own blood for my soul.

(Refrain)

My sin, oh the bliss of this glorious thought! My sin, not in part but the whole, Is nailed to His cross, and I bear it no more, Praise the Lord, praise the Lord, O my soul.

(Refrain)

And Lord haste the day, when my faith shall be sight, The clouds be rolled back as a scroll; The trump shall resound, and the Lord shall descend, Even so, it is well with my soul.

What makes a man go through that much pain and still acknowledge God's faithfulness and unfailing love? Spafford realized that every attack on his prosperity was an attack on his faith. "I wish that you prosper and be in health just as your soul prospers." Every attack on his wealth was an attack on his relationship with God. Every attack on his health was an attack on his relationship with God. This was why Job's wife said to him, "You have lost your prosperity, you have lost your wealth, and you have lost your health and you are still holding on to your relationship with God? Curse God and die" [Paraphrased]. I imagine that Job's wife wanted him to curse God and die so that she could remarry because he was useless to her. But Job refused. I pray that you will refuse to curse God. I pray that you will refuse to let your faith shake. I pray that you stand strong in your faith all the days of your life. Excellent leaders practice crisis anticipation and scenario planning. You must learn to practice crisis anticipation and scenario planning; if this then that, else this then that. It is like programming. You should always be mentally prepared for any setback because the enemy is thinking day and night about taking away your advantage. So, you must be at least a step ahead of the enemy. The enemy is strategizing on how to get you down, you must not be sleeping. You must be strategizing on how to frustrate his plan and his plans will be frustrated.

THE NEED

~ *You Are Only As Free As Your Well-Developed Alternative* ~

The need for security is one of the deepest needs we have. Once our security is threatened, that particular security treat preoccupies our mind. It is like we are unable to do anything else. Take someone that has just been promoted at work three times in one year. Imagine how confident he would be and how much spring he will have to his step. Then one day he bounces to work, and a little bird says the company is downsizing, sixty percent of the staff are going to be laid off. What do you think will happen to him? He will immediately begin to wonder if he is part of the sixty percent. He will consider sending out this resume and applying for another job. All because his financial security is threatened. He probably would not be able to do anything else until he gets that off his mind. Imagine someone that goes to the doctor for a routine medical checkup. He is not feeling sick or anything, it is just a routine check. The doctor just runs the usual tests and comes to him alarmed asking, "did you walk here or were you wheeled in?" That person's physical security is being threatened. Guess what happens? The strongest people usually begin to sweat because all of a sudden, his or her physical security is being threatened. Imagine after a God Will Do It Again Service [one of our special services in the church I pastor, God's Favourite House], you get home anointed and fired up, only to find three bats flying around in your room that was locked. You probably will spring into action immediately because you feel your spiritual security is being threatened. That is how we are wired as human beings, we need to secure our bases. God wants you to secure your bases.

To have proper security you must do four things. To have proper security, I must...

1. Prevent surprises from my own forces. You must prevent surprises from your internal forces. Remember the story of the Oba of Lagos, it is a classic example. You must prevent surprises from the people around you. There are four types of people around you; the first category are your confidants, confidants are for you. They may not fully understand your vision, in fact they may not even believe everything you believe but they are committed you as a person. They are the ones that are there for you when you are down and out. They are the ones that give you a listening ear when the world shuts theirs against you. Your confidants are your most precious possession on earth apart from the Holy Spirit. The second category are your constituents. They are not necessarily for you, they are for what you are for. Politicians understand this very well,

there are no permanent enemies or permanent friends, just permanent interests. Your constituents are for what you are for. When what you are for changes, they jump ship. The mistake a lot of people make is to think a constituent is a confidant. It is usually disastrous what happens when you take a constituent as a confidant. If their direction changes, they will throw you under the bus without even thinking. They will sell you for five pieces of silver. The third category are your comrades. They are not necessarily for you, they are not for what you are for, they are against what you are against. People usually erroneously marry their comrades because they have a common cause. Imagine two people that come from humble backgrounds, both fighting poverty and fall in love while the battle is on. Or one person is sick, and the other person is strong in faith, and they are both fighting a disease and fall in love in the process. The problem is that when poverty goes, and God blesses them with financial wealth, there is nothing else to fight so they face themselves and fight each other. That is the danger of marrying your comrade. The fourth category are your conspirators. The people around you that are not for you, they are not for what you are for, they are not against what you are against, they are against you. In fact, all they are thinking about is how to get an advantage over you. Let's say you have an office, all they are thinking about is how they will look sitting on your seat. Some people have made their conspirators their closest friends. It shows you how unsafe a lot of lives are. Prevent surprises from your own forces.

2. Ward off enemy invasion. We have spent a lot time on this already. Don't take anything for granted. Always assume your enemy is intelligent and competent.

3. Deny information to the enemy. Make sure there is no information leakage in your life that seeps to the enemy. If any information seeps from your life to the enemy, make sure it is false information. If an armed robber enters a house, takes the money and the valuables. Then just as he is about to go, he expresses his desire to rape someone and then asks if there are any women in the house. If you have a daughter upstairs or in

the back room sleeping, what would you say to the bandit? I bet you would say there are no females in the house. Would that not be a lying? No. There is only one answer to that question, there are no women in this house. Is that lying, to a robber? Note that this is not a license for people who lie. You need to know where to draw the line. The armies surrounded Elisha's house, they were looking for the prophet that had been leaking their war secrets to the king in Israel. They were telling Elisha that they wanted to kill him. What did Elisha say? He said, the person you are looking for is not here. Let me take you to where he lives. They were speaking to Elisha, but he said he was not the one and it was not a lie. But this is different from changing the figures on your tax returns. That would be a lie.

4. Maintain freedom of action. You are only as free and as secure as the options you have. You are only as free and secure as your well-developed alternative to whatever you are doing today. What are you doing today? You are only as free and secure as your well-developed alternative. You need to sit down and come up with a well-developed alternative to whatever you are doing today. Why? One of your most important life strategies should be the systematic development of options. This applies only to some areas but not all areas. What are your options? In soccer for example, over the period of a season, the team is only as strong as its bench. A team is only as strong as the options available to that team, every leader should know that. What are my options? You must have options. However, **the most secure places in God do not provide us with options**. Marriage for instance, your marriage is one of your most secured fortress. Your home is your fortress of protection, but God has not provided us with options in marriage. Once you are married, you are married; no "plan B". Regardless of what your spouse can or cannot do, there are no options. The most secured places in God do not provide us with options. Some people feel they are entitled to options because their current wife has only given birth to male children, because they believe that it is female children that take care of their parents in old age. Keep going, perhaps when you

are on child number ten, heaven will see your persistence and give you a female child. You have only one option and it is this woman that you have married. What if we are trusting God for the fruit of the womb, we do not even have children yet, what are our options? Ask Abraham, because of the option he took, Israel and the rest of the world are still suffering till today. If you do not have children yet, trust God who says, none will be barren in the land. The most secure places in God do not provide us with options. What if my husband does not have money and is not holding up his financial responsibility in the home? I acknowledge that this is a major issue in some homes. In fact, I have seen women that walked out on their marriages because their husbands were struggling financially. You have no options, stick with him! What if my wife is no longer beautiful, what are my options? You have none, that is your portion. The most secure places in God do not provide us with options. Another example is your calling, the gift and the callings of God are without repentance. It means God does not change His mind, He does not give you options and that is what it means primarily. If God has called you, He has called you. I was giving a minister an assignment and he said to me, "This assignment is hard, can I be a Jonah?" My response was, "For every Jonah there is a whale!" If God has called you to do something and you do not do it, God will do everything possible to bring you to your knees. I can share my own stories with you. As for me, I have chosen to go the "easy" route; whatever God wants me to do, I will do it because God does not change His mind. He is not making things up as we go. He has already said this is what you will do and that is what you will do. You are most secured in the center of God's will for your life. Guess what? It is right at the center of His will, even though there are no options, that is your most secure place. Jesus says the man that lays his hands on the plough and is still looking for options is not fit for the kingdom of God [paraphrased]. I say to my colleagues in the church office, we do not have job, we have a calling - two different things. So, we respond to our responsibilities as a calling.

The most secure place in all of creation is heaven. Heaven does not provide us with options. Heaven is not for everybody. Yes, Jesus if for everybody but heaven is not. God has said there is only one way to Heaven, no options. I used to have philosophical discussions with my dad, he said to me [did not know better at the time], that Heaven is like a market. A market has different entrances and he was breaking it down for me as he understood it. That was what I believed and embraced even though I was going to Church with my mum. Then I came across John 14:6 (NLT) "Jesus told him, "I am the way, the truth, and the life. No one can come to the Father except through me." I saw that my dad was wrong.

There are no options to the most secured places in God. I did a research some time ago on the world major religions -Hinduism, Buddhism, Judaism, Islam, and Christianity. In Hinduism, Krishna says that the truth is very elusive, to even gain access to the truth you have to chant, "Krishna Krishna rama rama Krishna Krishna rama Krishna...etc... and maybe you get a glimpse. But like a butterfly the truth can fly away." That was what Krishna said, google it, it is in the public domain. In Judaism, their key figure is Moses and Moses said in Deuteronomy, "Another prophet will come after me, Him should you obey." Moses was talking about Jesus. In Buddhism, Buddha on his death bed said, "I am still in search of the truth." In Islam Mohammed said, "I am just a prophet pointing the truth." But when Jesus showed up and said, "I am the way, the truth, and the life. No one can come to the Father except through me." There is no one else in history that laid claim to it. Jesus is the only way. The most secure places in God do not have options.

You may be struggling with Jesus being the only way. Or you may have embraced multi-lateral access to God like I did, handed down by my dad. Or you may have been with Jesus and you jumped ship and went back to the world. But today you see that your life is not safe. The Word of God says, "The Name of the Lord is a strong tower the righteous run into it and they are safe." I urge you to embrace Jesus and embrace the security of God for eternity. No time like now!

CHAPTER 7
THE PRINCIPLE OF UNITY OF COMMAND

The Principle of **Unity of Command**: For every objective, ensure unity of effort under **one** responsible commander.

~ One Person In Charge ~

Under the principles of war, unity of command means that all the forces unify under one responsible commander. It requires a single commander with the requisite authority to direct all forces in pursuit of an objective. In other words, it means one mission, one boss.

The significance of unity in any family, organization or team is indispensable for victory. Jesus said (Mark 3:25, NLT) "if a house is divided against itself, that house cannot stand".

An important aspect of unity of command is owning the objective. We all think and act differently based on our personalities, bent and experiences; therefore, we may not always agree completely with every decision. However, once a decision is made and the objective is clear, we owe it to ourselves and everyone involved to own the objective.

"But the Lord came down to look at the city and the tower the people were building. "Look!" he said. "The people are united, and they all speak the same language. After this, nothing they set out to do will be impossible for them!". (Gen.11:5-6, NLT)

Where there is unity of command, nothing is impossible. When a home, a business, a church, and even an individual is united and speaking the same language, nothing will be impossible. It is possible for an individual to be divided; for some people what is going on within is the opposite of what is happening without. However, when an individual is single, speaking the same language, what is going on within is what is going on without, nothing will be impossible.

God pronounces a huge blessing on unity. Psalm 133:1 (NIV) "How good and pleasant it is when God's people live together in unity! 2 It is like precious oil poured on the head, running down on the beard, running down on Aaron's beard, down on the collar of his robe. 3 It is as if the dew of Hermon were falling on Mount Zion. For there the Lord bestows his blessing, even life forevermore". The Easy Read Version and the Common English Bible translations put it this way, Psalm 133:1 (CEB) "Oh, how wonderful, how pleasing it is when God's people all come together as one!". That is why the enemy strives so hard to cause division, to bring di-vision [fantastic ideas that do not line up with the vision]. Some of us have people in our lives that are consistently in sync with the enemy. You have to identify such people in your life and ostracize them. The only way to deal with a cancerous cell is to cut it off.

Eze.11:19 (NLT) "And I will give them singleness of heart and put a new spirit within them. I will take away their stony, stubborn heart and give them a tender, responsive heart". The New International Version of Eze.11:19 reads, "I will give them an undivided heart...". Let this be your heart's desire and prayer. Unity makes you unstoppable.

Napoleon puts it this way, "Nothing is so important in war as an undivided command: for this reason, when war is carried on against a single power, there should be only one army, acting upon one base, and conducted by one chief." The principle of Unity of Command states that for every objective ensure unity of effort under one responsible commander. The key to the unity of command is one person in charge. If you check, you will discover that this is how God works. One person in charge is not only key to success in war but it is consistent with battle operations.

The Punic Wars were a series of three wars fought between Rome and Carthage. In the second Punic war, Rome had been invaded by the Carthaginians. At the time, Rome operated a senate system. It was clear to Rome that if they did not have a single person in command they were going to be wiped out by the Carthaginians. So, Rome appointed the famous Quintus Fabius Maximus as their commander in chief. But the senate of Rome gave him a six-month period to lead the nation. Fabius Maximus came up with the Fabian Strategy [also used in business management] and dealt with the opposing force of Carthage. For political reasons, after six months the senate appointed two generals to rule the nation of Rome alternatively. Immediately the Carthaginians got wind of what Rome did, they capitalized on it and defeated Rome. Rome learned a bitter lesson, one person in charge. Anything other than unity of efforts under one responsible commander will always lead to confusion and defeat.

COMMAND CENTRE

~ Establish A Single Line Of Command ~

If you check how God has structured leadership in the family, God always puts one person in charge. The husband is the head of his wife [Eph.5:23, KJV]. God did not put any conditions to that statement; He did not say it is the husband that is more intelligent, or the husband that is richer that is the head of his wife. That is just how it works, I did not put it in the Bible, God did! Mk.3:24 (TLB) "A kingdom divided against itself will collapse. 25 A home filled with strife and division destroys itself." God always puts one person in charge. When God was giving out the instructions at the Garden of Eden, He did not hand it over to a committee comprising of Adam and Eve. God gave the instruction to one person, Adam. It was Adam's responsibility to communicate it to his wife, which he did, but Eve fell out of the unity of command by rationalizing. Every time you rationalize a line of instruction, you are heading for trouble no matter how logical it sounds. Check the scriptures; when God wanted to save a whole nation, God raised a man – Moses, unity of command. When Moses' time was done, God told him to hand over to Joshua - unity of command. In Ezekiel 22:30 (NLT), God said I looked for a man to stand in the gap. God looked for one man to stand in the gap for a whole nation and that speaks of unity of command. Isa.6:8 (NLT) "Then I heard the Lord asking, "Whom should I send as a messenger to this people? Who will go for us…" [with emphasis]. With David and even with Jesus, it was one person in charge.

Thank God for giving us [men] really intelligent wives and God bless our wives. Ladies, never marry a man that you do not respect. Do not do it or you will be headed for trouble! Again, I say, do not marry a man that you do not respect just for marrying sake because when push comes to shove, you will not respect him enough to obey and align. If you have already married such a man, my advice to you is to align with him. God wants the man and his wife to reason together and to agree on a course of direction. But when there is a conflict in ideas and ideologies, God has set it up in such a way that there will be no confusion in the direction the family is going. My wife is very brilliant, I consider her more intelligent than I am, but I receive instructions from God. Men, it is your responsibility to receive a vision, a direction from God for yourself and for your family. It is your call. You have no business getting married if you are not clear on that instruction from heaven. If you are married already and clueless, my advice is go to God and He will give you your life instructions.

In the Book of Revelations chapters 2 & 3, you will see repeatedly, "Write this letter to the angel of the church in… Philadelphia, Ephesus, Smyrna, Thyatira, Pergamum…" John was obviously not writing a letter to an angel in heaven. The word angel in those scriptures means the messenger, the person that has spiritual oversight over that Church. God will always send His instruction to the person that has oversight. God does not send His instruction to a committee. I do not work with committees. We set up and work through teams for different purposes and teams are fluid. Anytime I set up a team, I am always clear who calls the shots. He or she may have been your junior in secondary school, but if he or she is the one calling the shots, you align – no stories.

Rom.16:17 (NIV) "I urge you, brothers and sisters, to watch out for those who cause divisions and put obstacles in your way that are contrary to the teaching you have learned. Keep away from them." God is showing us what to do with people that cause divisions. Watch out for people that are unable or unwilling to take clear instructions. God says, watch out for them and stay away from them.

Your job, as the leader, is to establish a chain of command. Each person should have only one boss and they need to know who it is. I recognize that everyone is a leader in different capacities, but each person should have only one boss. In a domestic setting, for instance in my home, the domestic staff have only one boss and that boss my wife. If she has a bad day and decides to fire one of them, I do not meddle with it. It is her business. You cause confusion when your wife has taken a decision and then you show up and reverse it. There is only one boss and that boss reports to you in the bedroom. In the bedroom you can ask her why she did things the way she did and attempt to set her straight. But when she steps out of the bedroom, who is in charge? In fact, one of the fastest ways of getting fired is not recognizing who your boss is. I have worked in organizations where people are dancing to the tune of people other than their line manager. When you enter any setting, it is your responsibility to discern who your boss is. Everybody has to be answerable to one person. My wife is in charge domestic of our domestic staff. If she decides to fire the cook, that is her business. As long as I have food to eat, I really don't care. God ALWAYS puts one person in charge!

Delegated authority is not diminished authority. Take a traffic warden at a crossroads for example; when the warden lifts up his hand to stop the oncoming vehicles, they have to stop. That is an example of authority and not power. The person that delegates authority retains the power but gives authority. If the oncoming vehicles refuse to stop, does the warden have the physical power to stop them? Not at all but the warden has the authority. As a child of God, God has given you authority. You have your line of command, it is clear, you have your authority from God. When you say, "in the Name of Jesus", do you know what that means? It means, "through the authority of Christ", I command you to go. The demon must go, not because you are powerful but because He is powerful. What should happen if the oncoming vehicles refuse to stop is, all the law enforcement agencies of the nation will be deployed to bring the vehicles and their drivers to book. This is very similar to what happens spiritually, and I need you to get this. When you enter a situation that is contrary to God, you stand as a child of God and you speak order into the atmosphere in the Name of Jesus Christ of Nazareth, there has to be order. If there is no order, all the law enforcement agents of heaven will be responsible to enforce that order. It is not your job! I have seen people rolling up their sleeves to cast out demons. Your job is to just speak the Word, as long as you are aligned.

Napoleon was legendary for his quickness of decision during a crisis, which always helped him maintain an unbeatable Unity of Command. As a leader, one things that tries to affect your unity of command negatively is crisis. Most people do not think clearly in crisis and as such they are unable to rise up to the occasion. Napoleon was legendary; he is clear and unperturbed in the midst of crisis and is able to give clear instructions. A research by Stanford University shows that the ability to function effectively in crisis is the most important single quality of a great leader. In other words, the most important single quality of a great leader [husband, church leader, organizational leader, or business leader], is the ability to function effectively in crisis. If the head of the home is always jittery and always negative when there is a crisis, it is a big problem. You have to be rooted in Christ so that when there is a crisis and everybody in the family is looking up to you, you can step up and give clear direction and God will back you up. Researchers discovered that the ability to deal with crisis could not be taught in classrooms, but only in crisis situations. In other words, there was no case study that could be used to effectively teach crisis management. One thing that is constant in leadership is crisis. A leader must be comfortable with crisis. Peter Drucker puts it this way, "The only inevitable event in the life of the leader is recurring crisis."

UNIFICATION

~ *A Deferred Instruction Is A Deferred Promotion* ~

For a Christian, to get to that place where in crisis and out of crisis, you are able to respond accurately, you have to be rooted in God's Word. You must align with the command center of heaven. Once you align, you take charge of your life. Jesus told a parable in Luke 19 about a master that gave his servants some money and after his return he asked for an account. He said to the one that did well "'Well done!' the king exclaimed. 'You are a good servant. You have been faithful with the little I entrusted to you, so you will be governor of ten cities as your reward.'" (Lu.19:17, NLT) Jesus said because you have been faithful in little, because you have taken charge of little, because you have risen to the occasion in little, I am going to promote you over a lot. Many people are asking God for promotion, but God is saying, have you risen to the occasion in the little, have you taken charge in the little? In the things of God, you cannot be promoted beyond your current level of obedience. What is your current level of obedience? That is your level of promotion, you cannot go past it. If God says do A and you do it, you get promoted. If He says do B and you do it, you get promoted. If He says do C and you do it, you get promoted. If God says do D and you logicalize it, heaven holds off the promotion. You may be praying - decreeing, binding and losing the promotion but heaven is actually waiting on you. The same things apply to who the leader in any setting delegates things to. If a leader assigns tasks to two people, one person does it and the other person doesn't but gave a "very good excuse". When it is time to assign someone to a higher responsibility, who do you think the leader will assign to it? The first person, without even thinking.

What instruction has God given you that is outstanding? Who has God told you to forgive but you have refused to move in that direction? What has God told you to give but you have decided to hold on to? For some of us the way to get back in alignment with heaven's command center is to repent. What do you need to repent of? God is convicting and confronting you with issues He wants you to repent of, but you are not repenting. One of the reasons people do not repent is they really want to go back, and repenting closes that door. You need to stop telling yourself that you will repent later because for every instruction you defer, there is a promotion that is deferred. In other words, a deferred instruction is a deferred promotion. What instruction is outstanding? Obedience is alignment.

If the work of Christ in a life does not align with the work the person does on the external, the person becomes fragmented. There is no unity of command in the person and as such the person will be conflicted. You have to ensure that what you are doing on the outside is completely aligned with the work of Christ on your inside. When the work of Christ on the inside aligns with what you are doing on the outside you become totally unstoppable. The issue is that a lot of us are living a double life; what is happening on the outside is different from what is happening on the inside, and that is where the problem is. To resolve this, many of us focus on working from outside-in. God does not want you to start from the outside. He wants you to resolve what is on the inside so that it can flow outward.

Gen.11:5 (NLT) "But the Lord came down to look at the city and the tower the people were building. 6 "Look!" he said. "The people are united, and they all speak the same language. After this, nothing they set out to do will be impossible for them!" The people God is speaking about in this scripture are aligned and because they are aligned they are unstoppable. When a home, a family, a business, a church, when a person is united it becomes unstoppable. Is there confusion in your life? Are you conflicted? I want to invite you to come under the command of God today where you will enjoy peace and have integrity. The word integrity is from the word integer. An integer is a whole number without a fraction. God wants to take away every fracture in your life and give you wholeness, so that you will be unstoppable.

CHAPTER 8
THE PRINCIPLE OF EXPLOITATION

The Principle of Exploitation: Follow up and follow through vigorously on an opening.

~ Do Not Give Up, Something Always Happens ~

You already know that life is a battle. You are the general of your life. You call the shots, so you have to be equipped. Every historical general we have looked at so far has deployed Scriptural principles to secure victory. It is also common knowledge that a lot of these generals are not believers. If they are deploying scriptural principles to secure victory, then we should be able to learn from them and learn from scriptures and deploy the same principles and secure our victory.

"I must work the works of Him that sent me, while it is day: the night comes, when no man can work." Jn.9:4 (KJV)

To exploit means to take full advantage of. Most people tend to think of exploitation as a negative word. Rightfully so sometimes because this world is full of people exploiting each other, or people exploiting the system and that is bad. Even a baby that is born innocent starts crying legitimately because of hunger... when the baby cries, everyone comes running to satisfy that need. The baby eventually discovers that this thing called crying is a weapon. In fact, it is proven that babies are better mind readers than adults. A baby can scan a room and read everybody's emotions. The baby learns very quickly to exploit the situation and even when the baby is not hungry the baby cries and get all the attention. The day the baby's cry is ignored, the baby changes its strategy. Capitalism is rooted in exploitation; while there is a good side to capitalism but there is a part of capitalism that is rooted in evil exploitation. Even spouses manipulate and exploit each other. For example, a lady knows her husband has had a long day and after his meal, all he wants to do is sleep. She patiently waits for that moment to pester him so that she can get her way. It is manipulation. Manipulation is like witchcraft. However, our focus in this chapter is not on the negative side of exploitation. The negative side I exists, but it does not take anything away from the positive side of exploitation.

I have friends that have really expensive phones but from my conversation with them, I can deduce that they do not know how to use even up to ten percent of its functionality. They are not exploiting the phone. They are not deriving full value form the phone. Why would you buy such an expensive phone if all you want to do is make and receive calls, perhaps send a few text messages and definitely take some selfies. Then what? That device you are holding in your hand is more powerful than ten mainframe computers of the 80's put together. Guess what? Those computers fill a whole room. The mainframe was used to send man to the moon and back, yet our smartphones are at least 10 times more powerful. We do not exploit what we have. I was in a friend's very expensive car, and I was just talking about the different functionalities and what the car could do. With every functionality I mentioned, my friend did not have any clue that her car could do any of such things. After a while I had to stop and all she said something like, "The car is fine, that is all I need." So, I suggest that she should spray her old car the same color as the new one and she insisted that she wanted the new car. But you are using just five percent of the car's functionality. You are not exploiting the car. What God wants us to do with our lives is to exploit and derive value from every gift, every talent, every relationship, every resource – everything He has given us so that at the end of the day He can say well done! Once we verify an opening, we are to follow up and follow through. The principle of exploitation simply states, follow up and follow through vigorously on an opening.

There was a time in history when the British forces came against the Turkish forces. There were twin battles, the first battle was called the battle of Dardanelles. Bottom line, it was a naval assault on Turkey. Turkey had aligned with the Germans; the British forces came against Turkey and bombarded Turkey through that channel – the waterway of Dardanelles. It was so bad that instruction had come from the political capital city, Constantinople to the Turkish general at the war front of Dardanelles to surrender to the British at twelve noon. Guess what happened? At 11 a.m., the British backed down from the battle. There is just so much to learn from that. If you tell a civilian at 8 a.m. to surrender to the opponent at 12 noon. The civilian will probably object to the idea of fighting for four hours, losing men in the process and putting his life in danger. Since we are going to surrender anyway, why not surrender now? That is how civilians think. But that is not how soldiers think. Soldiers follow instructions. The instruction was "surrender at 12 noon".

Surrender at 12 noon and at 11 a.m. the British general backed down. Turkey would have fallen but the British general did not follow through. Turkey stood because the Turkish general followed through on the instruction from Constantinople.

There was a follow up war at a place called Gallipoli. The campaign in Gallipoli is actually one of the greatest warfare disasters in the twentieth century. When the British discovered what had happened (backing down at 11 a.m. when Turkey would have surrendered at 12 noon), they gathered forces from Australia and New Zealand and launched a land attack on Turkey. They loaded thousands and thousands of men from their ship. If you remember the principle of the offensive, Napoleon will release them to battle immediately, right? But the British general delayed again. Turkey was totally caught napping, they were not expecting it. But because the British delayed, Turkey could regroup.

They waited for them on a mountain top and of course wiped out the British forces. They lost a hundred thousand soldiers in that battle because they did not follow through.

I pray that you will follow through. I pray that you will not stop at eleven o'clock when victory is just at twelve noon. I pray that if you were to give up at twelve noon, your enemies will surrender at eleven. I also pray that if you were unprepared for the attack, God will make the enemy to just perambulate until you are ready to wipe them out, in Jesus Mighty Name. I pray that when you show up before God there will be no door He opened before you that you failed to exploit. It is so instructive that we learn from these historical examples. Many times, God gives us an idea, a brilliant idea and perhaps we write it down, or tell a few people, or maybe filled it but we did nothing. Then time passed, you looked down the street and someone else has it executed that idea. In the past I would say they "stole" my idea. The truth is that they didn't. That idea implemented is a testament of your inability and my inability to follow through. If it was a business idea, as long as that business exists, it speaks to you about the day you did not follow through. What is that thing, that opening that God has given you? Follow through! What are you waiting for?

The Swizz are known for their wristwatches. The Swizz Chronological Institute came up with the quartz technology. The same quartz technology that is now being used on Casio and all the other brands. They came up with the quartz technology in 1960 but they put it aside because their preference was for wrist watches to have gears and mechanical parts. This was the only way to differentiate a hand-crafted wristwatch. The Japanese visited Switzerland and requested for the rights to the quartz technology and they gave the rights to the Japanese. Of course, you know what happened next, almost everyone in the world that has a wristwatch has one quartz wristwatch. The market that the Swiss dominated shrunk so dramatically. The point here is that the Swiss had it, God gave it to them [every good thing comes from God], but they did not follow through, they did not exploit the situation. I pray that your life will not be filled with regrets. My personal mantra is this; I am able to live with the fact that I have tried something, and it did not work. Than not try it and regret that if I had tried, it would have worked. I am able to live with the fact that I tried, and it did not work. Big deal! I will just try another thing. But a lot of people are laden with regrets of things they should have done.

Many times, we are faced with seasons that appear as if we do not get a break, no opening, and no opportunities. If you are in that category, the first thing you need to do is, remain faithful, the opportunity will come. Just stand your ground, **something always happens**. We shared the following quote previously when we were looking at the principle of security and I think it's worthy of being repeated...Bernard Baruch says, "When business is good, people believe that it will always be good. When business is poor, people believe that it will always be poor. Neither is correct." So, if you have been worrying about not having any opening or opportunity, stop worrying! Just stand your ground, something always happens.

During the second World War, there was a lot of pressure on Winston Churchill to negotiate with the Germans, but Winston Churchill refused. Everyone thought he was crazy because the Germans were on a rampage. Winston Churchill decided to stand his ground. Everybody knew, and he knew that the deciding factor of that war would be the Americans. Guess what happened? The United States of America said they are not going to participate in the war. But Churchill said, something will happen, and America will fight. True to it, something happened, and the Americans joined the war and the Americans determined the end of the war. Then people asked Churchill afterwards, how he knew that the Americans are going to join because he was so resolute. This is what Winston Churchill said, "I have studied history and history shows that if you persist long enough, something always happens." Do not give up, something is going to happen. It may look like everything is going to crash but just stand your ground because something is going to happen in your favour. Just stand your ground, do not shake. Something is going to happen and when it happens, exploit it!

THE SWITCHER

~ *Identify And Exploit* ~

The question is, what is the one thing that you can do right now to make things shift in your favour? It could be in your home, in your business, in your career, in your relationship with God, or even in your marriage; the question is what is that one thing you can do to make things shift in your favour in the face of open doors? Many people already know what it is. So my follow up question to you is, what are you waiting for? You know it is time to resign from paid employment and start up your own business, but you are enjoying the allowance. Are you waiting for your employers to kick you out? Propose to that lady, just open your mouth boy! What are you waiting for? Remember the story of my spiritual son I shared in chapter two when we were dealing with the principle of the offensive? What are you waiting for, pop the question? Worst case you will get a no, so what? Men live by 'nos'. Let me tell you my story; my wife and I had kind of been seeing each other for some time. Then she went in South Africa, so I picked up the phone, called her up and I proposed on the phone – action! She thought I was crazy, but she said yes and then called me back and said "No, you are crazy, I am not marrying you!" When she said no, I said so what, you will come back. I pursued my objective and the rest is history. Many men are afraid of 'no', why should you be afraid? 'No' just means try again, try smarter, try harder. Change your strategy, change the gear. It does not mean anything more so do not take it personal. Start the business. Obey God. God has spoken to you, God has given you an instruction, what are you waiting for? You know that you need to start serving in your local church, what are you waiting for? Exploit the situation. Some know they need to surrender to Jesus, what are you waiting for? Just surrender to Jesus and He will take it from there! What exactly are you waiting for?

There are four enemies of exploitation, four major things that keeps us from taking action and that keeps us from exploiting situations to our advantage. You can see them as switches to be switched off.

DELAY SWITCH #1: PROCRASTINATION

~ Every Opportunity Has A Day Time And A Night Time ~

We all know the famous, "I will do it tomorrow" response. You must have heard it said, that "tomorrow never comes". When tomorrow comes, tomorrow becomes today and no more tomorrow. Then it has to be tomorrow again. "I will take the exam tomorrow, or I will do it next week, or next month, or even next year." Many people have procrastinated their destinies, they have pushed it down the line. Just do it! You need to understand the characteristics of opportunities, also referred to as the nature of openings. There are three characteristics of openings, there may be more, but I want us to bring these three to focus.

1. **Opportunities Multiply As They Are Seized**. Everyone that has done anything great knows that many times all you see is an opening. But as you seize that opening, more doors open. It is as if multiplication just happens. Do not wait for the big doors to open. It does not work like that, you need to seize the little doors, then as you are walking into those doors the bigger doors will open. That is how it works. Opportunities multiply as they are seized.

2. **Opportunities Have Expiry Dates**. Jesus said in John 9:4, *"I must work the works of Him that sent me, while it is day: the night comes, when no man can work."* [KJV, with emphasis]. You may be willing to work but once it is night, you cannot. You may have all the energy in the world but once the night comes you can no longer work. Every opportunity has a day time and a night time. If you do not move while it is day, the door will be shut as soon as it is night and once the door shuts, it is shut. Every opportunity has an expiry date.

3. **An Opportunity Missed Can Hurt You For A Long Time**. Regret is the first point of hurt but this is way beyond regret. It can really cause serious pains. Esau missed an opportunity to retain his birthright. He paid dearly for it. There are some things

you do that the scars stay with you for the rest of your life. Israel missed the window of opportunity God gave them to possess the land. Israel did not get it back until a whole generation had died in the wilderness. That generation spent 40 years roaming the wilderness and did not enter the promise land because an opportunity missed can hurt you for a long time. The point is this, exploitation is so important, stop procrastinating and just do it. Have you seen a lady trying to kill a cockroach with her bare feet, no weapon in her hand? She just keeps go around and around in circles with the cockroach. It is not convenient but just do it, just crush it and stop procrastinating.

DELAY SWITCH #2: CAUTION

~ If God Were To Call The Qualified, No One Will Qualify To Be Called ~

Caution is not actually bad, but caution can become a problem. Caution is not necessarily fear. Caution is rooted in Logic and Systems. Logic meaning this makes sense. For example, we should be careful when we get to the edge so that we do not fall. It is logical, so it breeds caution. The other leg is systems, 'this is how we do it here'. While systems are good, and cultures are good; systems and cultures must be broken so that you can make progress. The system may have worked fifteen years but it is not working now, so break the system and create a new one. It is commonly said that "there can be no progress without change and there can be no change without challenge." You must be willing to challenge the status quo. A time must come when you have to set your caution aside in order to make progress.

The solution to logical caution is actually logic itself. Logic solves the problem of logical caution. An example in Scripture is the story of the four lepers sitting at the entrance of the city gates in Samaria in 2 Kings 7:3 (NLT) "…Why should we sit here waiting to die?" they asked each other. 4 "We will starve if we stay here, but with the famine in the city, we will starve if we go back there. So we might as well go out and surrender to the Aramean army. If they let us live, so much the better. But if they kill us, we would have died anyway." There was a slim chance that things will work out I their favour, so they took the chance and abandoned the logical caution and God rewarded them.

The solution to systemized caution is courage. There's a saying among the Yoruba tribe of Nigeria: "Let us do it how we have been doing it so that it can come out how it has been coming out." But the problem is we do not want it to come out the way it has been coming out. The story is told of a lady whose mum cuts her sausages up before frying it. The lady said "Mum, why can't we just fry the sausages whole? It is more enjoyable that way than cutting it up." The mother of course would not have it any other way but cut up. Why? This is how my grandmother did it, this is how my mother did, and this is how I do am doing it. In our family this is how we cut up our sausages. Then one day grandma came visiting and the lady was bold enough to ask grandma why they cut up sausages in this family as against just frying them the way they are. Grandma said, "In those days, our frying pans were very little, so we had to cut the sausages, or they would not fit into the pan." Things had evolved, development had advanced way beyond that and they now had bigger frying pans. But they were still cutting the sausages. Challenge the status quo.

You need courage. A lot of people prefer to wait for things to be perfect, 'dot the I's and cross the T's'. If you wait to cross all the I's and dot all the T's, by the time you are ready it will be too late. Reid Hoffman says, "If you are not embarrassed by the first version of your product, you've launched too late." If you see the first Twitter page when it launched, you would be ashamed of Twitter. If you had seen the first Facebook page, it was ugly, but Facebook shipped anyway. It is called incremental releases. I am a huge supporter of rapid application development, a software development paradigm. Which is, release the code quickly so that users will use it and let you know what the problem is instead of you staying in a cocoon, thinking you have all the solutions. But by the time you launch the solution, it does not fit. Guess what? God does incremental releases too. God does not wait until we are perfect before

He uses us. God does not wait until you are perfect, He just pushes you out there. You most likely would be screaming "I am not ready" at the top of your lungs but He pushes you out anyway. Then He sorts out this, sorts out that, then He does this and does that. Line upon line, precept upon precept, a little here a little there. Ten years down the line people look at you and say you are an overnight success. Yeah right! Or someone else says I want to do exactly what you did. Sure, try it.

God does not wait for us to be perfect before He calls us. He loves us too much to leave us the way we are of course, but He does not wait for us to be perfect before He calls us. God qualifies the called, He does not call the qualified. In fact, if God were to call the qualified, no one will qualify to be called. Everyone that feels that they qualify to be called will be a problem to God's work. The truth is that no one can stand before God's righteousness —none! So, be careful about who you want to give up on. Be careful about who you want to write off. Be careful! I have seen Christians write off other Christians. Be careful, do not be in a hurry to judge people because you do not know where God has taken them from and you do not know where God is taking them to. Ironically sometimes, it is the people that God has shown a lot of grace that are so impatient with other people. Someone comes to me waving a huge judgment stick over someone else. I just smile and stay quiet because I know where "Mr. Judgmental" here is coming from. How can you now be the person to pull out a judgmental stick, you? Very often, we write off people that God has tagged work in progress. Often times, we want to put a 'full-stop' where God has written 'to be continued, work awaiting completion'. Do not write off anybody.

DELAY SWITCH #3: DISTRACTION

~ *Move Swiftly On Opportunities But Stay On Track* ~

The third enemy of exploitation is distraction. Operation Barbarossa was a campaign launched in 1941 during the Hitler days. Hitler had three million solid soldiers that marched into Russia. In the first few months they had taken over 1.5 million Russian soldiers captive, not counting the soldiers they had killed. They were marching for Moscow, Joseph Sterling and his aides had already come up with a plan B, to abandon Moscow and escape, run for their lives. But Hitler saw Kiev, the capital of Ukraine, and Kiev was so tempting. Hitler and his men decided to take the city of Kiev on their way to destination Moscow. So, they encircled Kiev, a campaign called the Kiev encirclement. However, Kiev deployed the citadel strategy and pushed back. Even though the Nazi's eventuate defeated and conquered Kiev, by the time they were done their resources were depleted, the Russian winter had kicked in and they could not take Moscow. Kiev was a distraction.

While we need to move quickly on opportunities, we have to stay on track. Matt.6:22 (KJV) "The light of the body is the eye: if therefore you eye be single, your whole body shall be full of light." The word "single" in this scripture means healthy, clear, focused. What is distracting you? Identify it and get rid of it.

DELAY SWITCH #4: FEAR

~ Do Not Be Afraid To Step Up ~

A lot of people do not exploit the opportunities before them because of fear. In the parable of the talents [Matthew 25:14-20], the servant that did not take full advantage said "I was afraid I would lose your money, so I hid it in the earth. Look, here is your money back." Matt.25:25 (NLT). Fear can be a major challenge. A lot of us would have gone very far in life, achieved a lot of great things but for fear. People are afraid to take the steps to exploit situations. If you examine further what this same servant said to the master in Matt.25:24 (NLT) "...Master, I knew you were a harsh man, harvesting crops you didn't plant and gathering crops you didn't cultivate." In order words, he was calling the master an exploitative person. The master responded, "You know I operate the principle of exploitation, at least you should have put my money in the bank." [paraphrased]. God is showing us through the parable of the talents that He expects you and I to be exploitative. God expects us to get maximum results from everything He has given us. God expects results. So, immediately I learned that not exploiting your gifts, your talent, your resources, and your relationships is a major show stopper. Matt.25:30 (NLT) "Now throw this useless servant into outer darkness, where there will be weeping and gnashing of teeth.'"

God expects results, He expects multiplication. This servant returned to the master exactly what the master had given to him and he got into trouble. If all you do is protect your talents with your life and present it back to God just the way He gave them to you, I want you to know in advance you will be in trouble. God wants you to get rid of fear. Most people think that it is normal to fear and so no one can really live without fear. No, it is not. In fact, God has only one solution to fear, cast it out! 1 John 4:18 (NKJV) "There is no fear in love; but perfect love casts out fear, because fear involves torment. But he who fears has not been made perfect in love." Banish fear, cast it out, drive fear out totally. If you can successfully deal with fear, you will become almost unstoppable. Almost because there are other factors involved. Fear is one of the major things that keeps people grounded.

IBM approached Bill Gates and asked him to write an operating system for them. Bill Gates said, "Sure, right away!" Why is this so important? It is important because at that time he did not have an operating system. He did not even have the time to start writing an operating system. Writing an operating system is huge, even with all the tools available to us today. A lot of people would have been too afraid to take on the job, but Bill Gates took it on. He found a company in Seattle that had already written an operating system and bought the code from them for fifty thousand dollars. Bill Gates did not write the initial code for MS-DOS, he bought it and labeled it Microsoft Disk Operating System. He sold it to IBM and the rest is history. We often break our heads over things we can buy. Why reinvent the wheel?

Bill Gates was not afraid to take on the challenge. Do not be afraid to step up. Exploit the situation to the glory of God. Today, Microsoft is everywhere; like him or hate him, you have to respect Bill Gates. He took the step. So how can you know God and still be afraid to take the step. The door is open before you, what are you waiting for?

It is your responsibility to find that opening and to exploit it. Even if the opportunity is right before you, it is still your job to exploit it. There is a tendency for us to think that openings and opportunities will happen in the distant future. An Anonymous quote states that "The greatest people maximize the opportunity at hand." Look around you, there are opportunities before you already. Stop looking everywhere for what God has already given to you. It is there, see it. The story of Elisha and the widow in 2 Kings 1-7 [NLT] is very instructive. This woman came to complain to Elisha that the creditors had come to take her sons. Elisha asked her what she had in her house. Like the widow, many of us are quick to say I do not have anything. Then she remembers the jar of oil and Elisha said, we will work with what you have. The story, her story changed forever. What do you have?

In Luke 9:10-17 [NLT], Jesus told his disciples to feed the five thousand men, not counting women and children. Feed them? But we do not have anything! Jesus says, what do you have? Well, nothing except these five loves and two fish, a little boy's lunch. Like the little boy's lunch, a lot of us are looking at the opportunities before us and they look really small in comparison to the crowd in front of us. But Jesus said feed them because it is as you take the little opportunities, that the bread and fish will multiply. That is how it works. In Judges 6:11-16 [NRSV], the angel of the Lord described Gideon as a mighty man of war. Gideon said, that cannot be me you are talking about. There is something in you that you cannot see but God sees it because He put it there and He is calling for it. Mighty man of war, get up! Mighty woman of war, get up. God is saying you will have victory! In Exodus 4:1-5 [NLT], God said to Moses, you are going to deliver my people, Israel. Moses says how? God says, "What is that you have in your hand?" Moses say, "In my hand? It is just a rod." God said, "With this rod you will bring about deliverance!" My point is, you already have the opportunity that will change your life, it is in your hands already like Moses. Like Gideon, it is within you. Like the disciples, you have the relationships, the "little boy" in your life already. Like the widow, it is in your house already. God wants you to deploy it.

Acres of Diamond is a story of a farmer who had heard about how other farmers had become rich by discovering diamond mines. So this farmer sold his farm and with that money went on an expedition in search of diamonds. He spent everything but found nothing and he eventually jumped into the ocean and committed suicide. Meanwhile back home, the man that he sold the farm to was crossing a small stream on the property and saw a bright flash of red and blue light from the bottom of the stream. Apparently, the farm that farmer sold to go in search of diamonds was sitting on a diamond mine. Many of us are married to people that are diamonds, but you are looking for diamonds where it is not. For some others, like Gideon, your life is filled greatness, greatness resides in you, but you are selling yourself cheap because you are looking for diamonds. God is saying to you, it is within you. Like God said to the widow, it is in your house. Like God said to the disciples, you have the relationships already. Like he said to Moses, it is in your hands.

Follow up and follow through vigorously until you have fully exploited the opportunity.

CHAPTER 9
THE PRINCIPLE OF ECONOMY

The Principle of Economy: Never spend more men and resources than is necessary to achieve an objective.

~Count The Cost, Do The Math, Great Leaders Conserve Resources~

For there to be victory, there has to be conflict. Life is a battlefield, and as the general of your life, whether you will have victory or defeat depends on you (to a large extent). Not the nation, not the government, not the politicians but you, are the general of your life. The earlier you realize this, the better for you. The posterity of your soul, of your destiny, and of your generation is up to you. While we will vote people into government and the government has a responsibility to provide an enabling environment for the people. Yet the posterity of your soul and of your life is in your hands. Even in the countries that are considered the "best" countries, there are paupers. There are people that will not even become all that God has created them to be. The truth is that until the individual takes responsibility for his or her destiny, nothing happens – nothing! For instance, as a husband, whose job is it to make your wife happy and to love your wife? Is it the government's job? Whose job is it exactly? As a wife, whose job is it to make sure your husband fulfilled? Whose job is it to ensure that you prosper spirituality, you prosper in your souls, you prosper financially? Whose job is it? It is your job. The day you take responsibility for it, that day marks the beginning of your progress. In this chapter, as is consistent with the other chapters before it, we will be examining the different strategies and principles that have been deployed in ancient and modern warfare by outstanding war generals.

"But don't begin until you count the cost. For who would begin construction of a building without first calculating the cost to see if there is enough money to finish it? Otherwise, you might complete only the foundation before running out of money, and then everyone would laugh at you. They would say, 'There's the person who started that building and couldn't afford to finish it!' "Or what king would go to war against another king without first sitting down with his counselors to discuss whether his army of 10,000 could defeat the 20,000 soldiers marching against him? And if he can't, he will send a delegation to discuss terms of peace while the enemy is still far away." Lu.14:28-32 (NLT)

Jesus in this passage of scripture is teaching us the Principle of Economy. Count the cost. Do the math. Sit down and check every single variable. Do a proper assessment of your resources by asking the follow questions; Am I able to build? am I able to launch this attack? Should I fight this battle? Don't fight battles you should not be fighting. You do not have enough resources to fight every battle that comes your way. It's common-sense to avoid some battles. This is essentially what the Principle of Economy entails. General George Patton captures it excellently when he says, "Every battle we fight will result in a gain for us or we will not fight." In other words, we do not engage in battles when we are not sure of the outcome. One of the key reasons why you should commit your life to Christ is because the outcome has been predetermined. We can take on challenges being confident that the outcome has been predetermined. In our everyday lives, we would be confronted with battles and we will be confronted with choices to go to war or not to go to war. In your relationships, you will be confronted with the option to battle or not to battle. Stop and check first, should I be fighting this battle or not?

The battle of Asculum was fought in 279BC between the Greeks and the Romans. The king of the Greek, king Pyrrhus was very adamant to take on the Romans. So, he deployed a lot of resources against the romans and he actually won the initial battle. But after the victory, he made the popular statement, "Alas one more victory and we are lost". In other words, the cost of winning that battle was so much that they could not even afford to fight another battle. Guess what happened? The Romans came again, and Greece was devastated. The lesson here is this; not every victory is worth your while. In fact, some victories are actually defeat in disguise. Thus, the Pyrrhic principle evolved from this, the same Pyrrhic principle that you come across in business and in leadership. The Pyrrhic Principle states that Pyrrhic Victory is a victory that inflicts such a devastating blow on the victor that it is tantamount to defeat. Yes, you have won the argument, but you have lost the relationship. Yes, you have shown your wife how foolish she is and how knowledgeable you are. But you have crushed her so much that you are losing the relationship. My question to you is this, which is more important – the relationship or the victory? Such a victory is a Pyrrhic Victory. You have succeeded in squeezing money out of your husband, even the money he could not afford to give you. Yes, you got the "victory" but the man cannot trust you anymore. You may pride yourself with knowing how to squeeze your husband, but you have actually lost the relationship. You can apply this same principle to your children, to your colleagues at work, and to your boss. Do you actually think you have gotten victory? Think again! Is this issue so important that I will lose the bigger things of life? Is it worth buying the new bag and sleeping with someone you are not supposed to sleep with? Is that victory; the bag is the trophy for fornication and adultery? What about the blow it has dealt to your soul? Can you recover?

The Principle of Economy puts these questions at our door step. "Never spend more men and resources than is necessary to achieve an objective." When you have an objective as an individual or a family, the principle of economy says, never spend more men and resources than is necessary to achieve an objective. Great leaders conserve resources. Great leaders are willing to pass on an opportunity if they cannot justify exploiting it. Life does not only present us with battles, life presents us with opportunities. However, just as you are not meant to fight every battle, you are also not meant to take on every opportunity. Great leaders have a way of deciding which ones to pass on and which ones to take on. No matter how juicy the opportunity looks, the question is, should you engage?

FIRST PRINCIPLE

~ The Fact That You Have A Resource Does Not Mean You Should Use It ~

Life teaches us not to take on every opportunity that life presents. Every lady that comes to puberty has a menstrual circle approximately every month and that is an opportunity to have a child. The woman that insists on seizing all her opportunities to have children will literally kill herself. But God keeps bringing the same opportunity every month just to teach us not to take on every opportunity that comes our way. Great leaders know how to look at opportunities and immediately determine whether it is worth exploiting or not. This is important because critical resources are scarce. When you take on one opportunity, you are going miss out on another opportunity and you do not have enough resources to take on every opportunity. This is actually the first principle of economics; Critical resources are scarce. Time is scarce; no matter how much you fast and pray you cannot have more that twenty-four hours in a day. Talent is scarce. Money is limited. Gold is limited. You must always conserve and economize.

If you are in Nigeria be certain that people will call you "Ijebu". The "Ijebu" people are from western Nigeria. They are perceived to be very economical and thereby seen as stingy. They never pay more than necessary for anything - never! (The only exception is their flamboyant parties) I grew up with my grandmother and she was a traditional Ijebu woman. She never pays more than necessary, in fact I thinks she always pays less than necessary. One of the things I used to hate when I was growing up was following Mama [my grandmother] to the market.

In English language, pricing is the process whereby a business sets the amount at which it will sell its products and services. However, in Nigeria the process of determining what you will pay for goods or services is also called "pricing". Typical example, we get into the section for tomatoes sellers in the market and Mama will start from the first person. The person has priced the tomatoes for twenty Naira for example, and Mama will squeeze and squeeze until the person agrees to sell for twelve Naira. I am standing there thinking from twenty Naira to twelve Naira, great bargain, buy it. But Mama will not. Then she goes to the next shop and the sellers offer her fifteen Naira and she goes through the same process again. She says that other seller has agreed for nine Naira and I'd say to myself (I dare not voice it out) "Mama, the seller said twelve Naira not nine Naira". She would squeeze and squeeze until the seller agrees to ten Naira. Finally she will buy here, right? Nope! She always checks at least four stores and then most times she will go back to the very first seller to price again saying "I only came back because I like you, your competitor gave me at such and such a price but you have to match or do better than your competitor" and most time she gets the first seller (or whoever's tomatoes looks nicest) to sell at such a low price. I am carrying the bags as we "roam" around the market, so you can imagine my frustration, coupled with the fact that I usually would feel sorry for the tomato sellers and many times I'm ashamed to follow her back to the first seller. So, immediately I hear that Mana wants to go to the market, I am out of the door because I do not want to have to go through her "shameless haggling". But in that process, Mana was teaching me an invaluable lesson, that you have to economize your resources. There's no shame in it. The fact that you have money does not mean you should spend it. The only thing some people know to do with money is to spend it. If that is the case, then you are in trouble. You need to go and listen to one of my messages: Thinking Clearly About Finances [audio resource available FREE on the Thrive Podcast on iTunes by God's Favourite House].

A lot of us are familiar with Operation Desert Storm also known as the Gulf war in 1991. The late Saddam Hussein bragged that it was going to be the mother of all wars, but it turned out to be the mother of all defeats. The USA led allied forces bombarded Iraq, reduced it to almost nothing. All this was done economically. By the time the war was over, the allied forces had lost only two hundred soldiers compared to fifty thousand or more that Iraq lost, in such a short time! That is the principle of economy at its best. Look for opportunities to make your resources [financial, human, etc.] go further because being economical gives you options. As we said in the Principle of Security, you are only as free as the options you have.

ECONOMIZE

~ One Of The Signs Of Righteousness Is The Ability To Store Treasure ~

A certain man started up as a newspaper boy and became a billionaire in US dollars. When someone like that speaks, you and I should actually listen because there is something you can learn from such a person. His name is Clement Stone and he says, "A part of all you earn is yours to keep, and if you cannot save money, the seeds of greatness are not in you." The first time I came across this statement, it shook me to my core. I know that some people will immediately point to the fact that Jesus says we should store our treasures in Heaven where moth and robbers cannot get to. I know you store your treasures in Heaven by giving; giving to the poor and giving to God's work. I understand all that, but the truth is you cannot give what you do not have. If you have not learnt how to save how would you have to give? If God wanted you to take care of the hungry people around you for instance, and you have not been saving, how would you have to give? You would not have anything to give when God calls for a seed like He did to the Jews. If you do not have it saved, you would not have it to give.

Prov.15:6 (NLT) "There is treasure in the house of the godly..." In other words, you find treasure in the house of the godly. One of the signs of righteousness is being able to store treasure. It is in the Bible! Prov.21:20 (NIV) "The wise store up treasure and oil, but fools spend whatever they get". Economize! Ps.112:3 (NIV) "Wealth and riches are in their houses, and their righteousness endures forever." If you have no income for the next six one year, can you survive? Think about that.

In economics there are four pivotal concepts that reveal the human nature. These concepts show you and I how we make choices and show us [if we are wise] how to relate with the people in our lives. How we relate with the people in our lives determines how far we go. Our relationship determines our height. I am not an economist, I am a software engineer, but I read economics, government, politics, civil disobedience, etc... I read about all sorts of things but I focus primarily on what God has called me to. So, for better understanding of these four basic economic concepts I will tell you a story. As we go through the story, you will see these concepts jump out at you.

The first concept: imagine you have been given two job offers. One offer is for one million dollars per annum and the other offer is for ten million dollars per annum. Which would you choose, all things being equal (like the economist says). All things being equal which would you choose? You would most likely choose the ten million offer. From time immemorial, all things being equal, everyone will choose the job with the ten million dollar salary. People prefer plenty to scarcity. That is the first concept. People prefer More to Less; it is not bad to prefer more to less, it's only human.

The second concept: back to the story; so, you have chosen the job that pays you ten million a year. Then you are given the option of receiving your salary as a lump sum at the beginning of the year or at the end of the work year. All things being equal, which will you choose? Unanimously from time immemorial, man always prefers Sooner to Later and that is the second concept of economics. The nature of man always prefers sooner rather than later; It is not bad, that is just how we are. Whatever that thing is, you want it now! Husband – now! Money – now! Breakthrough – now! Everything – now - now, now! People prefer more to less and people prefer sooner to later.

The third concept: now imagine that at this time, you have two organizations offering you ten million per annum. Organization A requires you to clock in at six o'clock in the morning and clock out at nine o'clock at night. Organization B requires you to clock in at nine o'clock in the morning and clock out at half past four in the afternoon and in between you have a lunch break. Which would you choose, all things being equal? From time immemorial, people do not only prefer more to less, sooner to later, people prefer easier to more difficult. You need to understand this about human nature, that is how we are, people prefer more to less, people prefer sooner than later, and people prefer easier to more difficult.

The forth concept: the two organizations before you are both offering ten million per annum, they are both going to pay at the beginning of the year, and they are both easy-peasy. However, organization A is huge, and their cash reserve is amazing. The organization B on the other hand has had a history of intermittent cash flow problems. Organization B is struggling, but organization A has excess liquidity and they are both offering the same thing, which would you choose, all things being equal? You will choose the one that is more certain. So, people do not only prefer more to less, sooner to later, easier than difficult, people prefer certainty to uncertainty. Again, this is how we are wired.

As long as you are on earth, you are going to be dealing with people. What will give you the greatest joy in life is people. What is able to cause you the greatest pain in life is people. What is going to open the door to your next level is people. Everyone in your life and everyone you are in a relationship with (your spouse, your children, your boss, your employees, your customers) prefers more to less, sooner to later, the easier to the more difficult, and they prefer certainty to uncertainty. If you understand this, you will be a master at leading people and a master at dealing with people.

The marriage relationship for instance, is one of the closest relationships most people will have. What does your husband want? I am not going to tell you what it is but I can tell you that he prefers more to less. He prefers it sooner than later. He wants it easier than when you make life difficult for him before he gets it. You can be sure that he wants it certainly rather than contending with uncertainties. It is the same thing with women, what does your wife really want? Think about it, what is it? Let us say it is money for example, she prefers more to less. She prefers to have it sooner than later. Women can be patient, but everybody loves instant breakthroughs. She prefers to get it from you easier than when you make it difficult for her. I can tell you that she definitely prefers to be certain about getting it than uncertain. These concepts are the basics of economy and economics. Of course, there are others and the economist will tell us there are other building blocks. But these are the basics.

ACCELERATORS VS. DECELERATORS

~ *Victory Is Certain When Decelerators Are Replaced With Accelerators* ~

Unfortunately, the four basic natural economic affinities of human beings (mentioned above) can be destructive. Preferring more over less creates greed and greed is a destiny destroyer. Choosing sooner rather than later [instant gratification rather than delayed gratification], creates impatience. Impatience is a destiny destroyer. Wanting things to be easier rather than difficult creates laziness. Laziness is a destiny destroyer. Preferring certainty, over uncertainty feeds risks aversion. Risk aversion cripples our ability to take risks. Risk aversion is a destiny destroyer because every destiny will require you to take several steps of faith.

For you to have victory and fulfill your destiny, you need to turn these destiny destroyers to destiny accelerators. Firstly, replace greed with generosity. Generosity in place of greed accelerates your destiny. *Prov.11:24 (NIV) "One person gives freely, yet gains even more; another withholds unduly, but comes to poverty."* People think when they gather all they can then they will become wealthy. God Word says one person gives freely and gets even more, another withholds unduly and becomes poor. Greed will decelerate your destiny, generosity will accelerate your destiny. *"Give freely and become more wealthy; be stingy and lose everything."* (NLT) Look around you, there are people you can be generous to. Give freely and become wealthy. Replace greed with generosity.

Secondly, replace impatience with patience. Patience is a powerful destiny accelerator. People think when someone is patient he or she is losing time. Be patient. One of the most powerful people on earth are the patient people. Things are moving, people are talking, but they are not in a hurry. They are patient. Heb.6:12 (ESV) "so that you may not be sluggish, but imitators of those who through faith and patience inherit the promises." To inherit the promises of God, you need patience. It's not enough to have faith, you need faith and patience. To enter into your destiny in God, you need to be patient. You have prayed and fasted, but you need to be patient. Patience is a force of destiny. Impatience destroys destinies very quickly. A lot of people are full of faith but impatient. Impatience can reduce someone with a lot to someone with nothing. No farmer gets a harvest by consistently unearthing the seeds, checking if it had germinated. Do not be impatient. Relax, calm down, everything God has promised you will come to pass.

Generosity in place of greed, patience in place of impatience. Thirdly, Diligence in place of laziness. Diligence accelerates your destiny. Our major challenge as human beings is that we get satisfied too easily. God promotes you to that level you have been desiring on your job or He takes your business to the height you did not think was possible. Unfortunately, a lot of people begin to relax. The truth of the Word of God is this; as long as there is breath in your nostrils, you have not arrived. The day your assignment is done is the day you arrive, and they will take you to heaven. I am saying that it is possible to have all the money in the world and still not have arrived. There are still resources in mars and people are going to Jupiter. People are going to outer space these days, have you not noticed? I have friends, not that I know personally but I follow them socially, that are going to space.

WINNING

One of them particularly, he joined NASA because he wanted to go to space and when NASA did not take him, he created his own company. Today, he is giving people the space experience. People are colonizing mars and you are here fixated on earth. We have not even started. We get satisfied easily. I pray that God will give you a holy dissatisfaction because until you are dissatisfied with where you are, you cannot make progress.

Prov.6:6 (NLT) "Take a lesson from the ants, you lazybones. Learn from their ways and become wise...10 A little extra sleep, a little more slumber, a little folding of the hands to rest—11 then poverty will pounce on you like a bandit; scarcity will attack you like an armed robber."

Do not fold your hands. That does not mean not rest. By all means rest. However, if you are like me, twenty-four hours appears not to be enough these days. There is so much to do, so much grounds to take, there is just so much.

Generosity in place of greed. Patience in place of impatience. Diligence in place of laziness and fourthly Faith in place of fear (risk aversion). God wants us to fuel our faith. The ability to step into the unknown, to see the invisible, hear the inaudible, and do the impossible requires faith. It requires taking steps that everyone around you will think you are crazy. But you are being fueled by what you know that God has put in your gut. The more you are able to do that and do it in the right direction, the more your destiny will be accelerated. There can be no progress without risk taking. Even with God, you cannot make progress without taking risks. Heb.11:6 (NLT) "And it is impossible to please God without faith. Anyone who wants to come to him must believe that God exists and that he rewards those who sincerely seek him." [with emphasis]. You cannot even draw close to God and God would not even be real to you if you do not have faith, if you do not take risks based on the Word of God. The more you draw closer to God, the more God owns you, the more God can economize you and manage you.

In Luke 14:25 (NLT) *"A large crowd was following Jesus. He turned around and said to them,* 26 *"If you want to be my disciple, you must, by comparison, hate everyone else—your father and mother, wife and children, brothers and sisters—yes, even your own life. Otherwise, you cannot be my disciple.* 27 *And if you do not carry your own cross and follow me, you cannot be my disciple.* 28 *"But don't begin until you count the cost. For who would begin construction of a building without first calculating the cost to see if there is enough money to finish it?* 29 *Otherwise, you might complete only the foundation before running out of money, and then everyone would laugh at you.* 30 *They would say, 'There's the person who started that building and couldn't afford to finish it!'* 31 *"Or what king would go to war against another king without first sitting down with his counselors to discuss whether his army of 10,000 could defeat the 20,000 soldiers marching against him?* 32 *And if he can't, he will send a delegation to discuss terms of peace while the enemy is still far away.* 33 *So you cannot become my disciple without giving up everything you own."* While we can take the lessons from the words of Jesus and apply it to economy, it is also clear that Jesus was speaking about deeper things. He was talking about spiritual economy and the lives of the people.

In verses 25&26 [Luke 14, NLT], *"A large crowd was following Jesus. He turned around and said to them, "If you want to be my disciple…",* if you want Me to own you, if you want Me to economize you, if you want Me to be in charge of you, if you want to be My resource, you must hate everyone in comparison to me. Wow, Jesus is just amazing! Just in case you do not know who everyone is Jesus clarifies in verse 26 [Luke 14, NLT] *"…your father and mother, wife and children, brothers and sisters—yes, even your own life…"* People think that becoming a Christian is just a fad. But there is nothing further away from the truth than that. Becoming a Christian, a follower of Christ will change your life. Verse 26 *"If you want to be my disciple, you must, by comparison, hate everyone else—your father and mother, wife and children, brothers and sisters—yes, even your own life. Otherwise, you cannot be my disciple."* This does not mean you should hate everybody, Jesus says in comparison to Him. That means if you were to put your husband side by side with Jesus, and if you cannot choose Jesus over your husband then you cannot be Jesus' disciple. That is what Jesus is saying. If you cannot choose Jesus over your wife, you cannot be His disciple. If you cannot choose Jesus over your children, you cannot be His disciple. If you cannot choose Jesus over your brothers and sisters, you cannot be a disciple of Christ. If you cannot choose Jesus even over yourself, Jesus says, you cannot be His disciple. In verse 27 Jesus says *"And if you do not carry your own cross and follow me, you cannot be my disciple."* In other words, do not even start thinking about following Jesus "[Luke 14, NLT] *28...until you count the cost. For who would begin construction of a building without first calculating the cost to see if there is enough money to finish it? 29 Otherwise, you might complete only the foundation before running out of money, and then everyone would laugh at you. 30 They would say, 'There's the person...'"* who just quickly followed Jesus but could not follow him completely [paraphrased]. *"...who started that building and couldn't afford to finish it!' 31 "Or what king would go to war against another king without first sitting down with his counselors to discuss whether his army of 10,000 could defeat the 20,000 soldiers marching against him? 32 And if he can't, he will send a delegation to discuss terms of peace while the enemy is still far away. 33 So you cannot become my disciple without giving up everything you own."* Jesus did not say you cannot become His disciple without giving up a few things, or without giving up the crucial things, or without giving up the pivotal things of life. No, Jesus said we cannot become disciples of Christ without giving up everything – **Everything**! Wow! On the day known as Palm Sunday in the history of the church, otherwise known as the Triumphant Entry of Christ into Jerusalem, Jesus told his disciples, *"go and tell the man that tied the donkey and its colt that the master has need of it."* As He rode into Jerusalem, the people took everything, they took off their clothes and they laid it down shouting, *"Hosanna to the Son of David, blessed is he that comes in the Name of the Lord."* Do you want your destiny accelerated? Generosity over greed. Patience over impatience. Diligence over laziness. Faith over (fear) risk aversion. Jesus is saying everything.

CHAPTER 10
THE PRINCIPLE OF SURPRISE

The Principle of Surprise: Accomplish your purpose before your enemy can react effectively.

~Every Strong Man Has A Secret~

The definition of surprise is to cause to feel wonder, astonishment, and amazement, as at something unanticipated. God is able to surprise. Eph. 3:20 (KJV) *"Now unto him that is able to do exceeding abundantly above all that we ask or think, according to the power that worketh in us."* God can do exceedingly abundantly above all you can ask or think. God is able to surprise you and God is able to surprise your enemies. As the general of your life, you call the shots and it is your responsibility to understand these principles and deploy them to your advantage. It is your responsibility to understand and deploy the principle of surprise, unleash it to gain advantage. This principle of surprise works everywhere -at work, in business, at home, and in relationship. So how would one deploy the principle of surprise in a marriage relationship for example? Imaging your marriage has been experiencing a period of dryness and you have been having challenges generally. The only time I cook up a lie is when I am planning a surprise for my wife. I say to her let us go and watch a movie for example. Meanwhile I have bought a return ticket to Calabar (for instance). Then I drive straight to the airport and she did not get to pack anything. When we get to Calabar, she will go shopping for everything she needs and everything she will wear on the following day. Surprise! I can assure you the fire will come back suddenly! You can deploy these principles everywhere.

Women naturally like promises and men know this. If a man wants a woman, he promises her heaven and earth and she is always wise enough [not foolish enough] to believe. So, you hear phrases like, "Has he lied to you again?" because women just like to be spoken to. While a promise is good, a surprise is better than promise. Write that down, you will need it later.

The Principle of Surprise in warfare states; accomplish your purpose before the enemy can react effectively. In fact, most military campaigns are trigged by surprise. If you check historical warfare, most wars are trigged by a surprise attack. You will hardly find two nations sit down to discuss their surprise attacks. One nation will typically sneak and attack first because it is a principle of war. In 1950, North Korea attacked South Korea by surprise, almost took out the whole nation including the allied forces [the U.S. was behind South Korea]. But the military general of the United States also launched a counter surprise attack in what they called the Inchon Landing. The general of the U. S. army cut off the supply of North Korea and practically starved North Korea to death. With no water, no food, no medical supply, the war came to an end very quickly. In 1967, in the third Israeli Arab war, called the six-day war, Arab nations ganged up against Israel because the Arabs did not support the 1948 creation of the nation of Israel. Their objective was to wipe out the nation of Israel and leading this campaign was Egypt [south west] backed up by Syria [north East] and Jordan [East & south East]. Israel was surrounded. As they were planning to attack Israel, Israel deployed the Principle of Surprise on the 5th of June 1967, Israel attacked the air force base of Egypt, Syria, Jordan and rendered their air force useless. So, Israel had superior air power and by the 7th of June 1967, Egypt had surrendered, Israel had taken Gaza strip & Saini peninsula. By the 7th and 8th of June Israel had taken west bank and the old Jerusalem city and Jordan surrendered. By the 9th and 10th of June they had taken Golan Height, Syria surrendered. On the sixth day, by the 10th of June, Israel had won the war - only six days because they refused to allow their enemy to get ready.

Do not allow your enemy to get ready. Do the first attack. Before I got saved, I used to fight a lot and in street fighting there is a technique called "the first attack". If you are able to lunch the first attack effectively, you will most likely win the fight. In the Book of Joshua 6:1-27 [NLT], the children of Israel had been given an instruction to surround Jericho. They match round Jericho, the first day, the second day, the third day, the fourth day, the fifth day, the sixth day. The people of Jericho had no clue what they were doing. On the 7th day, they matched round seven times and gave a shout. As they gave the shout, the wall crumbled - Surprise! Israel took over Jericho. You must learn how to deploy the Principle of Surprise to your advantage. The two factors that produce surprise are <u>Speed</u> and <u>Secrecy</u>. Speed and secrecy produce surprise.

SPEED

~ When a Man is Hungry, Speed is More Important Than Quality ~

God expects you to move quickly. Once you are settled on the objective, move quickly - Speed. The popular writer of Art of War, Sun Tzu says, "**Rapidity** is the essence of war; take advantage of the enemy's unreadiness, make your way by unexpected route, and attack unguarded spots." For some people the best description of their lives is the phrase "Go-slow". It is a Nigerian term used to describe traffic. For such people everything crawls and drags, a perpetual slow pace. In the Name of Jesus Christ Of Nazareth, God will give you speed. Every baggage that has been weighing you down and preventing you from moving with speed will be lifted off your shoulder and the yokes will be destroyed, in the Name of Jesus.

Speed is so crucial in a lot of areas. *"When a man is hungry,* speed is more important than quality!" I tweeted this a while ago as an advice to ladies and got several interesting responses. When we first got married, the new bride [my wife] will get home early and would want to cook everything. Meanwhile, the new husband [myself] refused to eat launch at work so I get home hungry. So, this man comes home hungry and his wife is telling him about all the things she wants to make. At this point, I really do not care if the peas are well aligned on the rice, just give me something to eat. When I'm hungry, it is not important to me that the perfectly sliced tomatoes in an arc. Just give me something to eat, then she goes, "give five minutes". Every man knows that when your wife is in the kitchen and she says, "give me five more minutes" it translates to much more and feels much worse. Anyhow, those were early days, things have improved significantly. What I am saying is this, when a man is hungry, speed is more important than quality. You can apply that also to every area of your marriage [wink wink]. Similarly, in business, when your customers are "hungry" it is more important for you to deliver a working product first. Stop waiting to get a perfect product out.

Tom Monaghan was a pizza delivery boy for an Italian pizza outfit in the U.S. and every time he delivers pizza, he discovered that his customers were always edgy and never happy. When the customer is not happy, it affects his tip because an unhappy customer never leaves a good tip that is if they leave a tip at all. So, Tom took the feedback back to the team at the office, can we shorten this pizza production process? He went to management with the same proposal, but they said no. This is how pizza is made, it must go through this process before it is can be called pizza. Out of frustration he sold his second-hand car and started a pizza business. But his competitive advantage was speed. He gave his customers a thirty minutes pizza delivery promise and if he is not able to meet up with his promised delivery time, the customer gets the pizza for free. Guess what happened? The whole town began to order pizza from him with some hoping the pizza would not make it on time, so they will not have to pay for it. The business grew so big that its franchise is all over the world. The pizza outfit he started, Domino's pizza, took over the pizza industry in no time. Somebody discovered that speed is more important that quality, when a man is hungry. The caveat is, 'when a man is hungry'. The average man cannot taste the difference between Domino's pizza and the traditional Italian pizza. While the Italian will perhaps fuss over the cheese, the hungry man does not care and just needs to eat.

What do you need to accelerate in your life?

2 Samuel 23:15-16 [NLT], David said he was thirsty, and he wanted a drink from no other well but the one in Bethlehem. So, "the three" broke through the Philistine camp with speed, got the water, and broke through again on the way back with speed. With speed, you will be done before the enemy knows what you're up to.

SECRECY

~ Keep Your Mouth Shut ~

Secrecy is the second ingredient of surprise. In many cases, it is secrecy coupled with deception. Frederick the Great puts it aptly when he says, "Everything which the enemy least expects will succeed the best." What does the enemy least expect? That is what will succeed the best. If the action of an attacking commander is not conducted with complete secrecy, the surprise will be on him. If God needs you to execute something with complete secrecy and you do not execute it with complete secrecy, by the time you are executing it, the surprise will be on you. God gives you an idea, an instruction, a direction, an image; but many people have truncated a whole lot of things that God wants to do in their lives with their own mouths. We talk too much. God has just given you an idea and the first thing you do is to you call person "A" to passionately share the idea. Have you noticed that when you are done sharing, all of a sudden, the idea dwindles? It happened to me several times in the past but that does not happen anymore. I now know how to <u>keep</u> things, you have to know how to <u>keep</u> things.

I will tell you why the ideas dwindle from a spiritual stand point. When God gives you an idea, He expects that you *incubate* the idea. As you incubate the idea, you are generating spiritual power to birth the idea.

The more you talk about the idea before time, the more you are leaking the spiritual power that you need to birth it. At the end of the day, you would not have enough spiritual power to birth the idea. Secondly, sometimes talking about what God has told you, translates to putting the idea in the "spiritual public domain". When you do that, demons have access to it and that is trouble. You start fighting unnecessary battles. I mean no disrespect; you need to **keep your mouth shut!** Please, keep your mouth shut, it will save your life. Sometimes, this mostly occurs with a particular person. As soon you tell that person the idea, even if you do not tell anyone else, the idea will not see the light of day. Many people have such people in their lives and most times they know. So why do you keep talking to them about your ideas? Keep your mouth shut!

There is this folk tale about Alade, a successful man but had a problem. Alade's problem was that he had horns. Alade was a wealthy and well respected in the community but Alade always wore a big hat to hide his horns. Alade had this friend that he had really bonded with and he felt he could share his secret with him because he was confident his friend would not tell anyone. Alade called his best friend and said, "I want to show you a secret and it has to stay between you and I." so, Alade removed his hat and his best friend saw that Alade had horns. Alade's best friend could not keep it to himself. The secret was boiling inside of him. But he knew he could not betray his best friend which means he cannot tell anyone this secret. So, he went into an empty cave and he shouted, "Alade has horns!" and he felt relief immediately from the weight of the secret. Nobody heard, or so he thought. A tree grew out of that cave and the wood from the tree was used to make flutes for children. It just so happened that whenever the children play the flute, the only tune that came out was, "Alade has horns". So, the entire village found out that Alade had horns and Alade committed suicide. Yes this is just a folktale story, but the lesson is real. Keep your mouth shut!

Someone once said that "Never be angry with someone who leaked your secret. If secrets were easy to keep, you would have kept it to yourself." Funny but true. Keep your mouth shut!

Every strong man has something he has not disclosed, you can call it a secret. Every strong man has a secret. There are things that are only known between me and God, there is no human being on earth that knows them. As close as I am with my wife, she does not know. It is between me and God. People come up with all sorts of theories about "the secret of my power". Some people say the "secret of my power" is prayer, while others say it is evangelism. I hear all sorts and I just laugh because people are just clueless. There are levels of consecrations that God has with me, there are things for instance that other pastors can do that I cannot do. If you have such, keep it to yourself, keep your mouth shut!

Judges16:¹⁵ (NLT) *"Then Delilah pouted, "How can you tell me, 'I love you,' when you don't share your secrets with me? You've made fun of me three times now, and you still haven't told me what makes you so strong!"* Samson was a strong man, he had a secret, but he had a girl in his life – Delilah. Delilah asked to know his secret. Samson is a very foolish boy. He was dating a girl that more or less told him to tell her his secret so that she could kill him. He gave her false information and she actually planned to kill him. But because of the secret he had not told her, he over powered all the enemies she brought to kill him. And Samson kept on dating her. Then she tried again, and Samson told her something else and the she tried the third time and because he hadn't revealed his secret to her, she starts giving him attitude; "How can you say you love me when you have not given me the tools I need to kill you". That was what she said, does that make any sense? But Samson kept playing with fire. Stop playing with fire! Samson kept playing with fire until, the Bible says, "Delilah vexed him". For every Samson there is an ordained Delilah. Do not let Delilah terminate your destiny.

I was at the bed side of someone very dear to me just before he passed on. He was a solid man of God and he said to me, "Femi, I should have kept my secret, secret." My heart broke! They got him because he thought everyone around him loved him. He opened his treasury to everyone. Human beings are wicked. The Bible says, "the heart of man is desperately wicked". Do not jeopardize your destiny.

The God that we serve is a God of surprises. God always brings up surprises – always. Good surprises for his children; Eph.3:[20] *"Now unto him that is able to do exceeding abundantly above all that we ask or think"* (ASV). But bad surprises for His enemies; 2 Chron.20:22 (KJV) *"And when they began to sing and to praise, the Lord set ambushments against the children of Ammon, Moab, and mount Seir, which were come against Judah; and they were smitten."* God laid an ambush for His enemies. God was pulling off some serious gangster moves here. If you check the life of Jesus, it is filled with surprises. The way Jesus was born was a surprise. Surprise to Herod, surprise to Mary, and definitely a surprise to Joseph. Imagine being Mary's father and your young virgin daughter comes to tell you she is pregnant. Your head will probably spin in every direction at the same time. But after you have regained your senses, calmed down, you will sharpen your cutlass if you are a Nigerian man, and ask her to tell you who is responsible for getting her pregnant. Then she says, "It is the Holy Ghost!" How would you deal with that? When Jesus set out to pick His disciples, He chose sinners, the most unlikely people. What a surprise. His life was filled with surprises; he was dining with prostitutes and the scums of society. A famous prostitute even kissed His feet in public. The Bible says, she was kissing His feet and wiping it with her hair - Jesus, the Son of God? A holy man? He was filled with surprises. What did He do when He missed the boat? He walked on water. Surprise!

Even His death was a surprise, a surprise to the disciples because they thought He was going to restore the nation if Israel. His death was also a surprise to satan even though satan was responsible for His crucifixion. 1 Cor. 2:[7] (KJV) *"But we speak the wisdom of God in a mystery, even the hidden wisdom, which God ordained before the world unto our glory:* [8] *Which* **none** *of the princes of this world knew: for had they known it, they would not have crucified the Lord of glory."* None, not one of the rulers of this world knew what God had planned through Jesus. God is a master at keeping secrets and springing surprises. *"For had they known it, they would not have crucified the Lord of glory."* When they were instigating the people to shout, "crucify Him! crucify Him!", they did not know. When they were slapping Jesus, beating Him, and wiping Him, they had no clue. I can imagine the host of hell, everywhere tense and on the verge of expectation, watching and saying, "Nail this man to the cross, nail Him to the cross!" They thought they were about to get victory. They struck the nails through Jesus' hands. They waited, and they waited, the sun became black and there was an earth quake. Jesus said the words and then He gave up the ghost. The rejoicing began in hell, satan was sure he had finished Jesus.

I can imagine a huge party in hell, three days long, the celebration was fierce. But on day three, in the thick of the party, they heard a heavy foot step coming toward the party gates. Who could that be, they wondered. There was a quick head count, everyone was already present – demons, principalities and powers. So, who could it be? The devil nominated a demon to go and check. So, he ran to the gates, peeped and ran back to give this surprising report; "You would not believe it! It is Him!" "Who?" "JESUS!", the demon replied and as he said the Name of Jesus all of them somersaulted. "Lock the gates! Lock the gates! Lock the gates!" satan shouted. The gates were locked, secured and reinforced. When Jesus got to the gates, an angel blasted, *"Lift up your heads, O ye gates; and be ye lift up, ye everlasting doors; and the King of glory shall come in."* They attempted to challenge the instruction, *"Who is this King of glory?"* The angel announced, *"The Lord strong and mighty, the Lord mighty in battle."* Then the angel blasted the instruction again, *"Lift up your heads, O ye gates; even lift them up, ye everlasting doors; and the King of glory shall come in."* The devil and his hosts again tried to resist the instruction, *"Who is this King of glory?"* The angel blasted his response for the third time, *"The Lord of hosts, He is the King of glory!"*, and the gates crumbled. [paraphrased from Ps.24, KJV]

Jesus bruised the head of satan, He seized the keys of death and hell, and He led those in captivity captive. While He was on His way leading them to heaven, satan stammered and said, "but… but… but… I do not understand, you said it yourself, "It is finished"?" Jesus responded, "Yes, it is finished; sin is finished, sorrow is finished, confusion is finished, sickness is finished, poverty is finished, shackles and confinement are finished." When Jesus said, "It is finished" satan thought it is finished for Jesus, particularly when Jesus was buried. But God said, "No, He was just planted." For some, your situation appears as though that area of your life is buried. I am announcing to you today that it is not buried, it is just planted. The same Power that resurrected Jesus is entering your life now and is causing there to be a resurrection in your life. Everything that has held you captive up until now, in the Name of Jesus Christ of Nazareth, we command it to lose their grip. Everything that has kept your destiny, or a part of your life buried gives way to the resurrection power of Jesus now! The power of resurrection will bring you back to life. Sicknesses and shackles will be completely consumed as you believe. You will accomplish your purpose before the enemy can react effectively because of what Jesus Christ has done.

CHAPTER 11
THE PRINCIPLE OF SIMPLICITY

(In warfare) **The Principle of Simplicity**: Prepare clear uncomplicated plans and clear concise orders to ensure thorough understanding.

~Make It Clear & Communicate It Clearly~

Congratulations General, you have made it this far! I am confident that you will be consistently victorious. The way the Word of God works is you have to keep hearing it. Faith comes by hearing and hearing the Word of God. As you open your heart to God, He will do what only He can do in your life and in your situations, in Jesus Name. By now, I am certain that it is no longer news to you that life is a battle. However, since God has given you the promise of victory, as the general of your life, you must learn how to secure your victory. You call the shots and if you are going to have victory it is up to you. It is not going to be up to the witch in the village, if there is any. It is not going to be up to that wicked relative that is not wishing you well. It is not going to be up to that mean parent or guardian that has spoken ill about you. Neither will be up to your cousin. It is going to be up to you and the earlier you brace up and embrace that, the better for you. You are the general of your life! Say it out loud: "I am the general of my life."

Lu.10:[41] (NLT) *"But the Lord said to her, "My dear Martha, you are worried and upset over all these details!* [42] There is **only one thing worth being concerned about**.

Mary has discovered it, and it will not be taken away from her." This was Jesus speaking to Martha and He said, How many things are worth being concerned about? Only one thing! What was going on here and who was Martha preparing dinner for? Martha was preparing dinner for Jesus. Martha was not preparing dinner for herself, or for her boyfriend [if she had one], or for her husband, or her friends, her neighbors, but she was preparing dinner for Jesus. In preparing dinner for Jesus, there were a lot of things involved because you are not just cooking for Jesus alone, you have to factor in Jesus' company (His disciples et al). Martha was overwhelmed and stressed out. Jesus is teaching you and I that *the stress of life is not necessary.* All the stress, the activities, the hustle, the bustle we go through, Jesus says, is totally unnecessary. Jesus is saying. only one thing is worth being concerned about. Am I saying you should not be concerned about your health, worried about my finances, worried about the children, worried about your husband, worried about your wife? Absolutely. I did not say it, Jesus said so.

Jesus is a master of simplicity. He simplified life to only one thing, just one thing. If you can harness that one thing, all the stress in your life will burst and fizzle away. What I am sharing with you is not a theory, by God's grace, this is what is obtainable in my life. It is a constant state of <u>"no stress"</u> whatsoever, none! Do I have all billions of dollars? Not yet, but I have no stress, none. If I am tired it is because I have worked hard. I am not stressed out from worrying about things. Why? It is because that is the path way Jesus has shown me. You can live a life without stress, simplify your life! Martha, simplify your life.

A veteran war general, Gen. George S. Patton says, "Success in war depends upon the golden rule of war; Speed – Simplicity – Boldness.". In other words, the golden rule of war is speed – simplicity – audacity! We dealt extensively with speed in the last chapter. Audacity we learnt in the Principle of the Offensive. Simplicity is what this chapter is about. I have told you that I have the awesome privilege of pastoring an amazing church called God's Favourite House. At God's Favorite House, we have twelve core values and simplicity is one of our core values. As a people, we value simplicity and we are simple people. No need for the unnecessary, we keep it simple.

Prov. *13:*[7] *"A pretentious, showy life is an empty life; a plain and **simple life** is a full life."* (MSG, with emphasis).

There are so many fake people in the world today, and thankfully you will not find many fake people in God's Favorite House. If you find any, they are new and over time they will become simple. God says a pretentious showy life is an empty life. But a plain and simple life is a full life. Make it simple!

SIMPLIFY

~ If You Do Not Focus on Simplicity You Will Get Complexity ~

The simplest messages are the most helpful messages. I have listened to a lot of messages (teachings, preaching & lectures), the messages I find most helpful are the simplest ones. They are the most powerful messages. The simplest women are the most beautiful women, have you noticed? The ladies that paint their faces **excessively** and end up looking like masquerades actually put a lot of men off. The simplest women are the most beautiful. The simplest men are the most powerful men and they are the most faithful men. The simplest is always the strongest. The Principle of Simplicity states that *you should prepare clear uncomplicated plans and clear concise orders to ensure thorough understanding.* This is straight from a war manual. What the definition means in essence is, *let your plans be clear and communicate your plan clearly.* You can apply this principle across board. If you are running a business, what is the plan for that business? Make it clear and communicate it clearly. Does your receptionist know the plan for your business? Does the gateman know the objective of the business he is manning the gates for? Does your assistant know the objective? In your home, let your plan be simple and communicate it clearly. If I speak to your wife, will she be able to speak confidently about your vision and direction [plan] for the family? Do you have a clear plan, and has it been clearly communicated?

When you simplify your life, you take ambiguity and confusion out of the way. The mark of a great general is the ability to strip things down to their barest essential and then focus. If you are going to be a great general, you must learn how to strip thigs down. Take what is before you and simplify it. For instance, your children come to you overwhelmed about a lot of things. You can take their problems and simplify it. You spouse comes you overwhelmed and stressed out about things. You can take his or her problem and simplify it. That ability to take complicated problems and simplify it is the mark of a great general. It takes a lot of effort, but you and I must make the effort to eliminate every form of ambiguity and confusion from our lives. When you eliminate confusion, you minimize stress.

God wants you to be successful. However, as you go through life, you will discover that a major enemy of success is confusion. I believe you want to be successful otherwise you would not have come this far. The number one enemy of "the objective" is confusion and complexity. But the challenge with human beings is that we are naturally complex, which is actually a misnomer because God is simple. Since our God, our Maker is simple then why are we so complex?

Naturally, if you leave a human being, he or she will complicate things. If you do not focus on simplicity, you will get complexity naturally. Leave a child in his or her room, with everything well arranged, all the toys neatly put in their rightful places. In a few days, that room will be extremely complex with everything everywhere.

I have a colleague that used to be a master at complicating things. He has improved now though. Typical scenario, we need to move item A from location A to location B. So, I tell him what needs to be done and I tell him to come up with a plan. You would agree with me that the shortest distance between two points is a straight line, right? By the time he returns with that plan, it is as good as a maze. When I ask him, "can we not just move the item from point A to B without all the complexities?" he says, "I did not know that was what you wanted." It used to really crack me up. What else would I have wanted? It reinforced for me this truth that human beings are just naturally complex beings. Always prefer simplicity over complexity. If you do not strive for and you are not deliberate about simplicity, you WILL end up with complexity.

Simplicity, as simple as it is, is not trivial. It takes a lot of mental work. You can liken it to the process of digestion. You take in something and break it down. Digestion takes a lot of work but that is where productivity begins. Digestion "processes" the food and breaks it down to absorbable components: vitamins, minerals, glucose, amino acid, etc... At the same time separating waste product from nutrition. The waste products are passed out in urine and feces. Everything you eat has both the nutritious part and the waste product. That plate of delicious jollof rice has the **simple** nutritious part and the **useless & complex** waste product, no matter how delicious it tastes. The same goes for every idea, objective, plan, etc... It takes the process of "digestion" (a lot of mental work) to separate the simple from the useless and complex.

The Occam's Razor is a principle used in different fields to simplify things. Occam's Razor states that, it is pointless to do with more what can be done with less. This appears to be straight forward, right? It is pointless to do with more what you can do with less. But sometimes we just waste resources. Without casting aspersions at our ladies, but I have always wondered why women use an entire chapter to say something they could have said in just one sentence. Typical scenario, a lady has asked to see me because she needs help in some area. So, she shows up for the scheduled appointment and I am thinking, let us go straight to the point, so that we can spend a lot more time for the solution. So, I say, "just tell me what the issue is." Her response is, "I need to tell you what happened." "Alright, tell me what happened?" "That day, this person did…" and she starts to tell me a story. At some point I try to get things back on track because the cry for help sounded like she needed the help urgently. "Just tell me what the issue is." But she insists on telling me the whole story with all the actors, every single location complete with timing, not missing out a single detail. Believe me, that whole story could have been said in three sentences. By the time she's done we need to reschedule to properly address the issue.

Let me give you another example, my wife wants to tell me that she went to the grocery store to buy bacon, but since she did not find our regular brand, she bought what was available. Simple, right? But she starts with, "I entered my car and drove to the grocery story. When I got there, if you see the parking spot I found…" I am sorry, but I am not interested in the parking spot you found, just go straight to the point. She continues, "I went to the first isle, then I crossed to the second. Then I bumped into someone, you will not believe who." At the end of the day, I get the message which is she got the grocery. While that may be harmless when it comes to relationships and possibly helpful to connect with your wife and listen to all her stories. When it comes to resources, it does not make sense.

Do not spend more when you can spend less. This principle is used by detectives when solving cases, they take the direct approach. The simplest and most direct solutions are usually the most correct solutions. Medical doctors also use this technique when they are trying to diagnose a case, they take the direct approach. The programmers use it, the architects deploy it as well. Different fields that are into problem solving take the direct approach and simplify things. All significant progress in human endeavors [in science, technology, medicine, business, sales, marketing, etc.], has come from simplifying processes.

God is so simple that sometimes we miss Him. God is here, do you know that? He is here right now, beside you. Elijah needed to hear God, so he went up on the mountain. Lightening came, and he checked but God was not there. The thunder tore through the mountains, but God was not in the thunder. Then there was the earth quake, but God was not there either. He wrapped a mantle round his head, and he heard God in a still small voice. Most times we are looking for the dramatic, but God is there in the still small voice. We very often walk pass God without even knowing it because He is so simple. We get an instruction from God, but we do not even know it because God is so simple. Jesus is God, but He chose to come in a manger. He was so simple, they missed Him totally. The Bible says, He came to His own but His own did not receive Him". Why did they not receive Him? They were expecting a warrior.

If the God that made the heavens and the earth is so simple, why are we so complex? God says, if you want to be saved accept Jesus, repent of your sins, and the cross will avail for you. Some people cannot believe this is all they need to do to be saved. Do you want to be healed? The Word of God says, "you lay hands on the sick and they will recover." Many people cannot believe "it can't be that simple." They probably will believe if they were required to bring a goat, or a cow, or a turtle dove, or a three-legged mosquito. God is simple, and He wants you and I to be simple. He wants you and I to cut off all the confusion. Look at the different areas of your life and make up your mind to simplify your life.

How does anyone successfully simplify his or her life? I will teach you four ways I have learnt to simplify my life from God's Word.

THINK CLEARLY

~ *Do Not Be Average and Act Impulsively. Be Strategic.* ~

To simplify my life, the first thing I need to do is to think clearly. There is a whole lot of pressure, you are going through a lot, and you are really overwhelmed. Just stop and think clearly. Unfortunately, not many people think. A lot of people would rather have someone else do the thinking for them. Most times we want things to just happen, but God wants us to think, and He wants us to think clearly. Success is almost always the result of clarity. Think! Think!! Think!!! Concerning your business, sit down and think clearly. If you have a challenge with your spouse, sit down and think clearly. Just think! You have been having challenges with a particular child, just sit down and think. But do not just think, set your emotions aside and think clearly. It is great to have emotions but set it aside and use your brain. Think!

Human beings can be very impulsive. The average person acts impulsively. You do not have to be average. While the average person acts impulsively, God wants you to act strategically. God wants you to act based on clear thoughts, not based on what is thrown at you. You get into a situation, something is being thrown at you, God wants you to think and to think clearly.

Take a farmer dog for instance. When the farmer's dog gets restless and cannot seem to calm down, the farmer would take the dog to a large field that has rabbits. Once the dog sees a rabbit, it starts to chase that rabbit. But while the dog is chasing the rabbit, it sees another rabbit. The dog stops chasing the first rabbit and starts chasing the second rabbit. Then it sees yet another rabbit, it stops and starts chasing after the third rabbit and on and on like the that, the rabbits just keep popping out. At the end of the day, the dog is exhausted from the chase, but it has not caught a single rabbit. It is has used up all of its energy resource chasing and chasing. Interestingly, this is the story of a lot of lives. People are just chasing down rabbits but catching nothing. God wants you to live with intention, but you cannot live with intention if you do not have clarity of thought. You have to think, and you have to think clearly.

One of the most important life skills you can develop is the ability to focus **single-mindedly** on an issue. We all have things that distract us, legitimate things that distracts us. You need to cook for your family, you need to take care of your spouse, you need to take care of your children, you need to deliver results at the office, you need to be active in your community and the list just goes on and on. However, the truth is that those legitimate things will always be there. The ability to focus single mindedly on an issue and think it through is one of the greatest life skills you can ever develop. Sometimes I talk to folks that are worried and ask them a simple question and they say, "Oh, I have not thought about that!" What is the basis of your worry when you have not even thought through the situation? The first thing, you need to do to simplify your life is to think clearly.

THINK DIFFERENTLY

~ Identify. Focus. Simplify. ~

The second thing I need to do to simplify my life is to think differently. Imagine you have a business process (or whatever process) that is currently a ten-step process. Those ten steps are long and complex. So, you want to shorten the process to a four-step process and still achieve the same result. The thinking that produced the ten-step process needs to change. If you keep thinking the same way, you cannot get anything better. But to simplify that process, you need to think differently. You need to ask what can be improved upon? We all have our "ten-step" process in different areas of our lives. The mother in the house has her "ten-step" process to a pot of soup. Interestingly, it is possible for three different women living in the same house to each have a different process to the same kind of soup. One person may have twenty steps, while the other has ten steps and another five steps. But everybody will arrive at the same pot of soup. If you want to be efficient, you should think of how to shorten those steps and to shorten it, you need to think differently.

Everyone knows you need to do certain things to get certain results, but the question is, what can be improved? Look at your tasks and ask yourself, what can be improved? Examine every area of your life and ask yourself, what is that one thing that can bring about a dramatic change. In your job for instance, what is that one thing that can bring about a dramatic change? In your marriage relationship, what is that one thing that can bring about a dramatic change? When you discover what it is, the next thing is to focus and acquire the skills that you need to achieve that one thing. Take a marriage situation for instance; What do you think is the one thing a husband needs mostly from his wife? It is respect. Sometimes, I almost burst out laughing in my sessions with couples because no matter what twists and turns there are to the story, it amounts to the same thing. The man says to the woman, 'you do not respect me.' The woman is convinced the man has a self-esteem issue. Men, what is the one thing that if you do it to your wife, it will change the game? Love, but not just love, women want to feel loved. The man claims not to know what the woman is talking about because as far as he is concerned, he is trying his best. It is the woman that cannot be satisfied because she wants an arm and a leg. No, she does not. She wants to *feel* loved.

Love your wife, how difficult can that be? When I discovered that this is one thing that will change the game in my marriage relationship, I made it my all-consuming passion. I love only one woman; I simplify my life. A lot of men are not very versatile at loving their wives because they are like the farmer's dog, chasing different rabbits and catching none. Be focused; if you make loving your wife your focus, she automatically becomes your object of study and analysis. I have studied my wife, I know her – her body language, her non-verbally communication, her signs – everything! …ok, *almost* everything. I may ignore it, but I know what it means. When a woman is focused on her husband, it changes the game. If you can successfully respect your husband, you will change your marriage totally. If the man gets home and feels like a king, you will change your marriage totally. So, what should you be doing? Let that be your obsession. How can I make this man feel like a champion? Think, ask questions, study and analyze him.

Marriage counselling sessions can be very interesting. The man is saying, he does but feel respected, but the woman responds that "there is no man in the world I respect more than my husband, these are just plain insecurities speaking". At that point, what I usually would do is pick up a snack. It could be anything, from an orange to a cookie. Whatever it is, I eat it with such passion that the couple becomes quiet and all their attention is on me. At that point they are both probably wondering, why is this man eating like this. I turn my attention to the woman, and I say, this apple is very sweet, and she says, "is it?" After a while, I say this apple is rather sour. I see the confusion on her face and before she gets over it, I say in fact this apple is salty. At that point, she knows I am getting at something. Then, I say to her, you cannot prove me wrong because you are not the one tasting the apple. I am the one eating this apple and I am the only one that can tell if it is salty, sour or sweet. Your husband is the one receiving the respect that you think you are giving, if it is real respect who should know? The man. As long as he does not feel it, you have not given it (all things being equal). As long as your wife does not feel loved, you have not done it. The simplest way to find out if your wife feels loved or not, is not to pride yourself but to actually ask her. That is how you will know. Most times you would not even need to ask, just by interacting with her you would know.

What is that one thing you need to crack that will change your game at work, in your business, in sales, in service? Identify it and make it your obsession, your all-consuming passion. Do not stop until you crack it. Eccl.10:[10] (NLT) *"Using a dull ax requires great strength, so sharpen the blade. That's the value of wisdom; it helps you succeed."*

HANDS OFF

~ What Are You Really Accomplishing? ~

The third thing I need to do to simplify my life is to hands off. To hands off is to delegate or to outsource. Delegate internally or outsource externally but hands off. Hands off from what exactly? The question is what is the one thing that only you can do and only you should be doing - in your life, in your home, in your marriage, on your job, and in your business? Outsource [delegate] every other thing and focus on that thing **alone**.

You can apply this across board in different areas of life. When you first started the business, you were everything. But you have been running that business for a while, so why are you still doing your bookkeeping? That is the job of an accounting firm; outsource it and let them do it. It brings simplicity to your life. In the home, same thing, if you can outsource sweeping your compound, please do. But please do not outsource caring for your spouse because there may just be a connection between the care giving and you know what. Find the things that only you can do, then delegate and hands off the rest. I look at every leader and I assess them based on this. There are certain things only the leader can and should do. Identify it and outsource every other thing. Outsourcing is hands-off but eyes-on, you are still responsible so keep your eyes on it but take your hands off.

In Exodus 18, Moses was the new leader of the nation of Israel. Moses was doing everything - the decision making, judging the people - everything!

Ex.18:¹³ (NLT) *"The next day, Moses took his seat to hear the people's disputes against each other. They waited before him **from morning till evening**.* ¹⁴ When Moses' father-in-law saw all that Moses was doing for the people, he asked, *"**What are you really accomplishing here?** ...*¹⁷ "This is not good!" Moses' father-in-law exclaimed. ¹⁸ "You're going to wear yourself out—and the people, too...¹⁹ Now listen to me, and **let me give you a word of advice***..." [with emphasis]. (Please read the rest of the story)

You and I need to confront ourselves with this same question that Jethro put before Moses. What are you really accomplishing working from morning till night? Many people are just working, but they are not productive. A lot of us could do more with our time and get better results with our time. Pay attention to sound words, determine what only you can do, and back off from the rest. That is what I do; even when my colleagues bring an issue to me, I mandate them to solve it and send them back. They have to think and come up with options for resolving the issue on ground and then we can take it from there. If I have to solve the problem for you then I am doing your job for you. I do not want to do that, I want to do what only I can do.

In Acts of the Apostles chapter 6, the early Church discovered that the Church had grown, and they could no longer be involved in every detail and still fulfil the call on their lives. People needed to be fed and widows needed to be taken care of, so they approached the people with this proposal. Choose for yourselves men that are faithful and filled with the Holy Spirit. What they were saying in other words was, we are delegating this responsibility. We need to give ourselves to prayer and to the ministry of the Word, every other thing will be outsourced. So, think about your life, think about your home, think about your relationship, think about your business, and think about your career. What do you need to hand off and keep your eyes on? I am an entrepreneur and I have had to deal with a lot of entrepreneurs. One of the major challenges of entrepreneurs is finding people that are faithful, people that are trustworthy, people they can actually hands-off to. It is as if when you hands-off, they either attempt to make off with your business, or to destroy it. I know that it is a challenge, but you have to believe God that your case will be different. You have to believe God. I believed God, and in my business, I have good people. In ministry, I have good people. I have pastor friends that when they visit the church, one of the recurring questions is how did you get these good people? I say, I do not know but I believe that there are good people because you will have what you believe. If you believe everybody is a thief, you will keep attracting thieves, and they will keep coming after your money. But if you believe that God has people that have good hearts, God will bring people that have good hearts to you. Find the things that only you can do and hands-off everything else.

CUT OFF

~ *The Greatest Antidote to Stress is Simplicity* ~

To simplify your life, the first thing you need to do is **think clearly**. The second thing you need to do is **think differently**. The third thing you need to do is to **hands-off**. The fourth thing you need to do is **Cut-off**. Some things actually need to be put to rest [cut-off]. There are things in our lives that we must let go of. Many of people have what is called the "pack rat" mentality. "Pack rat" mentality is seeking to hold on to everything regardless of how much you currently possess. For some, no matter how full their wardrobe is, they want to hold on to that dress or that shoe. Your house is over flowing with things, but you still want to keep that couch. Why are you keeping that dress? "Just in case I need it", have you ever heard that response? You have not worn the shoe for the past eighteen months and you are still holding unto it "Just in case". The just in case way of thinking has a lot of people trapped in the "pack rat" mentality. So, I want to challenge you to get a box, sweep through your wardrobe, sweep through your room and under the bed. Some people have so much stuff under their bed it is unbelievable, and these are not people that have space issues. Everything you have not used in a reasonable number of months, those things you keep thinking "just in case" you need them some day. It could be a wedding gift; some people have been married for twenty-five years and they still have unopened gifts from their wedding day that they are saving, "just in case".

Pack everything that you have kept "just in case" and put it in that box. Label the box "my just in case box". For some of you a box is not enough, you need to a trailer. Feel free to mark that trailer the "just in case" trailer. For some, they have had three, four, or five children that are now all grown up. You are approaching fifty and you are still holding unto a baby pram "just in case" there is a retirement benefit baby. Pack your just in case toys, just in case shoes, just in case baby clothes, just in case bicycles, just in case electronics, just in case stuff. Put them together and label it "just in case", please do it today. Will you do it? Then take everything you have labelled "just in case" and find people that actually need them and give it out. God will bless you for it; and "just in case", God will be there for you. That is what you should do. That is what I do.

Just do it; examine your work space, your business, your homes and ask the question, "Why am I doing this?" Challenge the process. There was a Fortune 500 company, this company about six top level staff. The least paid among this group of six earns a six digits salary in USD. One of their major function is to come up with a 300 page report which they submit to the executive vice president every month. One day, the leader of the team began to ask, "Does anyone really read this report?" He asked in a none threatening way and he discovered that not a single one of the reports gets read month after month. So, he assembled his team and told them he was going to close that department. He assured them that no one would lose their jobs. He was going to put them somewhere else where they can be useful. After a couple of months, at one of their top-level meetings, someone said, "what happened to those monthly reports we used to get?" He said, "We discontinued it" and the person said, "It is a good thing you discontinued it, nobody reads it." That was the end of it. What are you doing that nobody cares about?

At the church I pastor, there are so many things that we have put to sleep. One example is our weekly bulletins; we used to print bulletins every week. The amount of resources that go into getting those bulletins out every week was a lot. Structure, content, proof reading, it was a lot. Many hours of my work week went into ensuring that the bulletins came out as expected. Then there was the cost of printing it every week. So, one day, I sat down with my team and said, "Are people really reading these bulletins?" One person said people like our bulletins. I said, "Are you sure?" I proposed an experiment, we would stop printing bulletins and see if anyone would miss it. We stopped and nobody missed it. About three months after, I walked up to a man in church and asked, "How was your bulletin last week?" He said, "Last week's bulletin was so powerful… your people are really doing a good job!" I did not say anything, I did not need to. I just walked away quietly and that was the end of bulletins in our church.

You cannot just do things because other people are doing it. That is the fastest route to killing yourself. You have a good hairstyle on that you made one week ago. Now you want to remove it because you have seen someone else's own. I hope you would not go bald. That is the fastest route to killing yourself. Do you know how many hours I have saved in my week and my colleagues' just from cutting off bulletins? What do you need to cut off?

Sometimes, it is actually a relationship that you need to cut off. If you are honest with yourself, there are certain relationships you are in that can best be described with the word "stress". Cut it off and see how stress free your life will become. When you have friends that only talk to you when there is "gist" [gossip that is], cut them off. The greatest antidote to stress is simplicity. At some point in my life, I made up my mind that I was going to have only one phone. Why should I be going around with five phones? Sometimes I want to call a person and after looking the five phone numbers of his/her contact on my phone, I get confused about which number to call. I have to call my assistant to tell me which one to call. Simplify your life! Some people have five phone numbers and they can tell you which one goes for what category of people – that is so complex.

The day I stopped receiving emails on my phone and cut-off social media from my phone, I believe it added years to my life. I just felt longevity added to me. It is amazing how much control our mobile phones have over us. Every time the mobile phone beeps, there's a compelling urge to look at it and as soon as that happens we are distracted from what we were doing. It just complicates your life. Most times, my phone is on silent mode. If I have to check my emails, I go to my laptop. When I shut my laptop, that is it, no disturbances!

Lu.10:⁴⁰ *(NLT) "But Martha was distracted by the big dinner she was preparing. She came to Jesus and said, "Lord, **doesn't it seem unfair to you** that my sister just sits here while I do all the work? Tell her to come and help me." ⁴¹ But the Lord said to her, "My dear Martha, you are **worried and upset over** all these details! ⁴² There is **only one thing worth being concerned about**. Mary has discovered it, and it will not be taken away from her."*

How many things are worth being concerned about? Only one thing! How many things are you trying to juggle? Jesus is saying only one thing is worth being concerned about.

When you discover and make your relationship with Jesus the center of your life, you position yourself for a stress-free life. When you make your relationship with Jesus the center of your life, every other thing is determined your relationship with Jesus. Before you take that job, how will it impact on your relationship with Jesus? Before you relocate to that place, how will it impact on your relationship with Jesus? Before you make that decision, how will it impact your relationship with Jesus. You need to hands-off and cut-off everything that does not help your relationship with Jesus. I have seen people take amazing job offers that led them out of their place in God. I have seen their souls become famished; in fact, they are practically backslidden. What will it profit a man if he gains the whole world and loses his own soul? Ask yourself this question.

I believe that God will satisfy you with long life and all. But if you had just three months to live, how would you spend your time? Think about it. Will you still be chasing all these things that are stressing you right now? The promotion you want to kill yourself about, will it be important? This business that you are depriving your wife and your family, sacrificing them on the altar of success, will that really be important? If you had just one, two, three months to live, I can bet it would not be so important. What are the things that you will really want to spend your time doing? Those are the things you should really be spending your time doing. You will want to get closer to God, right? I would want to get closer to God. You would want to make peace with people. You would want to spend time with your wife, you would want to apologize for not loving her more. You would commit to lavishing your love on her every single day of the three months. You would want to say to your husband, "I should have paid more attention to you!" You would want to listen to every conversation and indulge every single hug your children ask for. The truth is, that is how you should be living now. That is what cuts off stress, simplifies your life, and makes you powerful, unstoppable, and indestructible. The truth is if you had just three months to live, you would *think clearly*, *think differently*, *hands-off* some things and *cut-off* unnecessary things. This is how to un-complicate and to simplify your life! God is simple, simplify your life. I pray that God will give you the grace to simplify your life, in Jesus Mighty Name.

CHAPTER 12
THE PRINCIPLE OF CONCERTED ACTION

The Principle of Concerted Action: *Unify* and *bring* **all elements** *of your force to work together* **simultaneously** *in the achievement of your aims.*

~ *Your Personal Relationship With Jesus Is Your Greatest Asset On Earth~*

Our victory voyage began with the Principle of the Objective and key to the objective is **Clarity**. Next, the Principle of the Offensive; in summary, **Dare to Go Forward** [dare to make progress]. The Principle of Mass focused was on **Concentration of Forces**. Next, the Principle of Maneuver and the key to successful maneuvering is, **Be Flexible**. Next, the Principle of Intelligence; and key to intelligence is **Gather and Accurately Interpret Information**. The Principle of Security led us to **Cover Our Bases**. Next, the Principle of Unity of Command puts **One Person in Charge**. Then the Principle of Exploitation; key to exploitation is **Follow Up and Follow Through**, do not let any opportunity go by. Next, the Principle of Economy and key to economy is **Preserve Your Resources**. Then the Principle of Surprise led us to **Do the Unexpected**. Next, the Principle of Simplicity and key to simplicity is **Take the Direct Approach** – simplify! Are you ready for the Principle of Concerted Action?

Matt.18:[19] (NLT) *"I also tell you this: If two of you agree here on earth concerning anything you ask, my Father in heaven will do it for you. [20] For where two or three gather together as my followers, I am there among them."*

One of the greatest life skills you can have, is the ability to work harmoniously with other people. The ability to work in sync with the people around you is one of the greatest force multipliers. A force multiplier is something that magnifies your effort and giving it a larger impact. I can tell you several stories of military campaigns were a smaller coordinated force, defeated a much larger uncoordinated force. The fact that you are "small" does not mean that you will lose. If you understand how to organize your forces, you can win in spite of your size. A smaller military force working seamlessly with speed can and most likely will destroy a much larger and less coordinated force.

The Principle of Concerted Action simply states, unify and bring all elements of your force to work together simultaneously in the achievement of your aim. Ensure that things work in tandem with each. The ability to work in unity with people is so powerful. Skill for skill, I would much rather work with someone that can get along with other people than somebody that cannot. In fact, every organization will choose people that are team players over their colleagues that are lone rangers, skill for skill.

Great generals are only great because they have excellent officers at every level of command. This is also true about great organizations, beyond the great leadership, there are excellent people making things happen. No one does it alone. Everyone needs the help of other talented people. You need help, and so do I.

God created man in His own image, and He gave man everything he needed. But God looked at man and God said, "this man needs help" and God gave man help. Is it not ironic that most times when God gives us help, we say to God, "The help you have given me has caused me trouble!" Is it not ironic that when God brings you in relationship with people, instead of bringing the best out of it, you cause problems for them? Then you go to God and claim the people are giving you trouble. God says, "Not at all, that person's purpose is to help you".

Concerted action is the key to synergy. You cannot have synergy without pulling together. Synergy simply means, as far as human effort is concerned, one plus one will always be greater than two. However, you cannot have synergy without concerted action. The Scriptures say, "go to the ants and learn". Have you seen ants moving in a line? I like to disturb their formation for fun. Guess what? They still find their way and they are still maintaining their order, they are still in sync, they are still in synergy.

For a lot of people, the missing key is synergy. As Christians we are super blessed and rightly positioned because we have the supernatural benefit of something I like to call "synergy on fire!" What we have goes beyond natural synergy. Synergy on fire is aptly captured in Matt.18:[20] (NLT) *For where two or three gather together as my followers, I am there among them.*" Supernatural things can happen when we gather because Jesus is present - people get healed, people are set free. Just worshipping Jesus breaks chains and shackles off of us. The difference between the church and a social club is not the music, or the preaching. The difference between the church and a social club is not the choir, or the singing, or the worship. The difference between the church and the village meeting or the social club is the presence of Jesus. The presence of Jesus is a huge force multiplier for us. Even as individuals, when a man has synergy with the Lord, he has a huge advantage already. When you are in sync with the Lord, just you and God, you have a huge advantage already. The presence of Jesus takes our synergy to supernatural dimensions.

When you see someone that appears to be able to do more than what is normal or usual, it goes without saying that there is someone else helping that person. For instance, by the time you wake up in the morning, your five-year-old son has washed your car and even re-parked it facing the gate. He left the engine running and the cooling on [or heater depending on where you are] so that the car is good to go. When you get there and see your car, what thought would cross your mind? You would be certain that he did not do it alone, someone must have helped him. How could he reach the top of the car? He is not tall enough to have his feet on the pedals and look above the dashboard at the same time. Guess what? So you rightly conclude that your visiting sister helped him.

God is going to help you in a way that when people see the results, they will say, "somebody helped him/her, this could not have been by her effort alone." This is what God's Word says to us in Josh.23:[10] (NLT) *"Each one of you will put to flight a thousand of the enemy, **for the LORD your God fights for you**, just as he has promised."* What will make the difference in your life is, the Lord your God is on your side and He is fighting for you. Take Samson for example, just one person, he killed a thousand Philistines. The Philistines knew that he had a secret because it is not normal for one person to kill a thousand men. Even if the person is really strong, perhaps he will kill ten men from the enemy camp. But by the time he is done, he will be exhausted and will most likely be captured alive. Only one man killed a thousand men with the jawbone of a donkey. The philistines knew that there was more to Samson, so they sent Delilah. You need to know that Delilah is after you. Why? It is because the enemy knows that there is more to you than this. God is helping you.

Your personal relationship with Jesus is your greatest asset on earth and the enemy will come after it. The reason he is after it is simple, so that he can remove the "super" from your supernatural and make you natural. Once the "super" has been removed, you are in trouble. I pray that the "super" will not be removed from your supernatural. If you are reading this and you do not have a relationship with the Lord, today you must have synergy with Jesus. So that you, one person, can put to flight a thousand. One person chasing a thousand is beautiful by itself. Two people will put ten thousand to flight. God says, when two Christians come together, and they are in synergy [in sync], victory is inevitable.

The reason the enemy does not want you to be in any real fellowship and real relationship with God is because he wants to take you out.

The enemy knows that when you begin to link hands and forces with other Christians, he has no other option but to leave you alone. This is so powerful.

Deu.32:[30] (NLT) *"How could one person chase a thousand of them, and two people put ten thousand to flight, unless their Rock had sold them, unless the LORD had given them up?"*

God shows us clearly in scripture that the reason only one person can chase one thousand, and two people can chase ten thousand is because God makes it happen. This exponential effect and result can only happen because God made it happen. God wants you to link hands with His children so that together we will become unstoppable.

Matt.18:[19] (NASB) *"Again I say to you, that if two of you agree on earth about anything that they may ask, it shall be done for them by My Father who is in heaven. [20] "For where two or three have gathered together in My name, I am there in their midst."*

The question is, who are you praying with? If you are not praying with anyone right now you have limited yourself. God wants you to be unstoppable. Why do you think marriages are under such pressure? If husbands and wives can agree, they are practically unstoppable. If you are married, I am praying, in the Name of Jesus Christ of Nazareth, that every wedge between you and your spouse will be broken and God will cause you to link hands as you really should.

No one can do life alone. A major key to greatness is the ability to get along well with many different kinds of people. In my years of pastoring, I have met many different kinds of people. You have to have the capacity to ignore some shenanigans. Everything you accomplish in life requires the active cooperation and participation of people. Think about it, you needed people to accomplish everything you have accomplished till date. How did you get married? Many of us met our spouses through someone or in a community of people. How did you get your job or that promotion? Somebody put in a word for you. How did you come into this world? Two people came together and BOOM, you were born. There is always someone that God needs to use to help you get to the next level. The only time the devil is successful at executing his plan to destroy someone, is when he successfully pulls them out and keeps them isolation. It is his standard practice, I have seen this happen over and over. It is the enemy's standard pattern and painfully effective.

When you pull out one log from a bonfire, it still burns for a while, so it is arrogant, full of its own ways. But guess what? Slowly but surely the fire will die out and when that happens, flies and algae show up on the wood. There is protection in community. The more capable you are at getting along with people, the happier and more successful you will become. Rudyard Kipling captures it aptly when he says, "The strength of the wolf is the pack, and the strength of the pack is the wolf". A pack of wolves is extremely dangerous but the source of the strength of that pack is the individual wolves.

Now that you have seen the weight of concerted action, I am going to give you four keys to unlocking concerted action in your life. Four keys to deploying concerted action and making it work in your sphere of influence.

CANDID HEART

~ *Love People and Use Things. Not Vice Versa* ~

To unlock concerted action, you must have a **Genuine Concern For People**. You have to realize that people are not fools, they may not say anything, but they know when you are taking them for a ride. You think you are smarter than everyone else, so you playing games thinking you have bamboozled others successfully. People are not fools, the only reaction you may get from them is a smile if they are wise. For you to unlock concerted action, you must have genuine concern for people. Stop trying to use people; do not make the mistake of trying to use people, instead love people.

We are to love people. We use things and love people. Sadly, for some people it is the other way around. They love things and use people. You need to realize that people are not fools. Have genuine concern for people. I heard this said some time ago, I do not know who to credit it to, but it is a popular saying: "People do not care how much you know until they know how much you care." Even in your home, you will discover that your children do not really care how much you know until they know how much you care. You can be the greatest software engineer in the world, but until your spouse knows how much you care they really do not care how much you know. To unlock concerted action, you and I must have genuine concern for people.

SELF-ESTEEM

~ *It Is in Lifting People Up That You Are Lifted & Become All That God Has for You* ~

To unlock concerted action, you and I must **Have A Very High Self-Esteem**, and this is really important. One of my favourite pastimes is studying great men and women, regardless of their faith. One common denominator [and this is a huge thing] in great men and women is that they like themselves and they respect themselves. In essence, they are comfortable in their own skins; and because they like and respect themselves, they are able to like and respect other people. You cannot give what you do not have. If you hate yourself, you are going to hate other people. If you stand in front of the mirror and you do not like who you see, it is going to flow into your relationships. The people asked Jesus what the greatest commandment is. Jesus says, "That is easy, the greatest commandment is love the Lord your God, with all your strength, with all your might, with all your soul. This is the first and the greatest commandment" [paraphrased]. Then Jesus goes to say in Mark 12:[31] (NLT) *"The second is equally important: 'Love your neighbor __as yourself__.' No other commandment is greater than these."* The second is equally important, love your neighbor as yourself. You cannot begin to love your neighbor if you do not love yourself. Jesus says no other commandment is greater than these. Amazing!

Love your neighbor as yourself; you cannot love anybody more than you love yourself. The people that are able to love other people easily are people that have come to know who they are in God and love themselves. Hurting people hurt people. Loving people love people. If all you do in your relationships is scar and pull people down, then you are to be pitied. Great men always lift people up. Small men always pull people down. When the people you are in relationship with [your spouse, your children, your neighbors, your colleagues] consistently feel put down by you, they will not want to be around you. When you put people down, it also shows that you have very low self-esteem and you need to address it.

You need to see yourself as God sees you. Embrace God's love for you, become all that God has for you, and it will overflow into your other relationships. Do not be a crab. They say the reason the fisherman or the crab seller never have to worry about covering the crab basket is because no crab escapes. How so? The moment one crab attempts to climb out of the basket, the other crabs will pull it down. You need to get rid of the crab mentality.

There are people in your life, people you are in relationship with that God has brought your way so that you can help them become all that God has created them to be. So, stop pulling them down – STOP IT! It is in lifting people up that you are lifted and become all that God has for you. In my earlier years of pastoring, I struggled with giving people what I have. One day, someone asked me for information, and I struggled because I did not want to tell him. But I overcame the struggle and I told him. When he left my office, God said something I had never heard before. He said, "Every time you share what I have given you, I will give you four times more". I was like, "Every time? Wow!" So, guess what now I do? I am very eager to share what God has given me. It is small thinking really that makes people hoard things. Then one man of God came to my office, he said, "I have attended your God Will Do It Again service... tell me how you prepare the anointing oil." I remembered what God had said that every time I share what He has given to me, He would multiply it by four. So, I told him how I prepare the oil. As he stepped out of my office, the Holy Spirit showed me a higher level. The Holy Spirit said, "Now, this is how you will be preparing the oil going forward." Now you know why I am so passionate about teaching.

It is a small mind that thinks it needs to take away from others to become great. The only person that needs to die for you to fulfil your destiny died two thousand years ago, His Name is Jesus. You must have a healthy self-esteem.

Treat everyone below you exactly how you would want them to treat you if you were below them. Who is below you? Perhaps a house help, treat your house help the same way you want him or her to treat you if you were the house help. It would change your life. I know some people will struggling with this, and I know that is really hard, but this is the path way to your freedom. My advice to you is, treat your driver the same way you would want him to treat you if you were his driver. While we pray and believe God that we will only experience promotions and never regression, but guess what? Your driver can become the president tomorrow because God is a Master at taking people from the dunghill and setting them among princes. So, what if he becomes the president tomorrow? It is great that you are the boss but treat your staff as you would want to them to treat you if the roles were reversed. Put this in your mind every time you relate to people. I know you really want to slap him or her, and they probably deserve to be slapped. But before you do, ask yourself, if I did this would I want him or her to slap me? Remember Jesus says in Mark12:[31] (NLT) "... *Love your neighbor **as yourself**.' No other commandment is greater than these."* Therefore, treat everyone below you exactly how you would want them to treat you if you were below them.

FOCUS ON CONTRIBUTION

~ Contribution Makes You Valuable ~

For you to unlock concerted action, the next thing to do is **Focus On Contribution** and not on collection. Contribution makes you valuable and people treasure what they consider valuable. Imagine you have two friends; friend "A" always calls to ask for money and anytime you hear from friend "B" it is mostly a text notification from your bank telling you friend "B" just transferred some money into your account. He does that three times a year and when you call to thank him, he insists he is the one that needs to thank you. Let us say you have simplified your life, instead of carrying two phones, you have opted for a dual SIM phone. Then your phone rings one day, friend A is calling on one line and friend B is calling on the other line. Be honest, whose call will you pick? Even if you are Jesus Christ; Jesus said, "if you are ashamed of Me on earth, I would be ashamed of you before My Father." In other words, how you treat me determines how I treat you. Everyone appreciates people that go the extra mile, everyone! So, give!

If I experience a loss, I always ask myself two questions; the first question is, do I have an issue with my tithing? God says when I tithe, He will rebuke the devourers for my sake. So, I check my tithe and by God's grace, that is usually not the problem. The second question I ask myself is, am I holding on to something I should have kept where thieves cannot reach? God says that when you give, you are storing up treasures in heaven. But when you hold on to something on earth that you should have credited to your account, then there is bound to be a loss. For instance, God tells you to give someone a pen. When you obey and give, the pen gets credited to you in heaven. But when you hold on to the pen, you are holding on to something that does not belong to you. It qualifies for stealing. That pen automatically carries the tag, "steal me" on it. I know this may be really tough to take in for some people, but it is the truth of the Word of God. If God gives you an instruction to do something and you do not do it, that thing is marked for consumption. So, you might as well give it or you risk losing it. Like my people will say: "kuku give it."

I want to give you a project, an assignment. Make a list of all the important people in your life and determine, by yourself, what it will take for them to be happy in their relationship with you. Whatever it takes is your contribution, make the contribution. Who are the most important people in your life? Your spouse, your children, your siblings, your boss, close friends – take time out to sit down and list them. Then take them one after the other; what will it take for your spouse to be really happy to be in relationship with you? Write it down because that is your contribution. Now that you know what your contribution is, do it. What will it take for your boss at work to be excited every time you step into the office? That is your contribution, make it! You will see how people will turn in your favour. It is not just about praying for or receiving favour. You cannot continue to behave like a vagabond and be claiming and receiving favour. Contribution makes you valuable and people treasure what they consider valuable.

BETTER TOGETHER

~ None of Us Is Stronger Than All of Us ~

To unlock concerted action, you and I must realize and understand that **None of Us Is Stronger Than All of Us**. This just wraps it up nicely. You must realize that none of us is stronger than all of us. None of us is more anointed than all of us. Even if you are super strong, as soon as another person adds their "little" strength to yours, it will still be more than your super strength alone. Imagine you have thirty billion dollars in your account and someone else has a hundred dollars in their account. When you come together, and that person adds their hundred dollars to that thirty billion dollars, it becomes more than what you had initially.

Community is structured in such a way that you always have upward vertical relationships, downward vertical relationships, and horizontal relationships. The challenge is that many people do not know how to respond to and in the different levels of relationships. A lot of people want to pull themselves out of community maybe because the people in their horizontal relationships are always competing with them or vice versa. The downward vertical relationships usually require you to be responsible for the people you are in relationship with and some people do not want to be responsible for anybody.

Some people do not know how to respond in the upward vertical relationships. They refuse to submit to anyone, and no one can tell you what to do. Such people will have problems with God. With God, you need to get under the things that God has put over you. So that you can be over the things that God has put under you. The reason is, if you do not stay under the things that God has put over, you will not be above the things that God has put under you.

An old Chinese saying states that, "He who would rule must learn to obey." Unfortunately, so many people are jeopardizing their great destiny because they want to be law unto themselves. Let me illustrate with something that happened long ago. I think I read somewhere that the most important meal is breakfast. So, when I got home, I said something like this to my wife "I hereby decree that in this house there must be breakfast". Honestly, my wife is fantastic, all she said was alright I will do it. But for some reason, maybe because we had been used to a particular pattern of life, she did not have the strength to do it consistently. Then I would get angry and rock the boat. Then she will start again, and then stop again. I got so frustrated, and when I get frustrated, I report people to God. I am sorry if that does not sit well with you but that is what I do. So, I reported the situation to God, I said something like, "Lord, see they are not obeying Your constituted authority in this house. It is Your authority I have, and they are not obeying it" and I went on and on. Can you guess what God said to me? I can never forget it; He said, "You want breakfast, right?" I said, "Yes Sir, it is the most important meal in the day." Then He said to me, "Where is My own breakfast?". "You have breakfast?", I wondered. He said, "You wake up in the morning and you do not bow before me." Eureka! I did not tell my wife anything. So, the first time I did it, as I woke, I rolled off the bed. As I was rolling, my wife was trying to catch me because she did not know what was going on. I said, "Leave me!" I rolled off the bed and hit the floor on my face and I began to worship God. Guess what? My wife began to get up and to make breakfast by herself.

When you get under the things that God has put over you, you will be able to get over the things that God has put under you. This is so powerful, and we all need to get it. You must have the ability to identify an instruction because in a community an instruction can come from downward vertical relationships. God can use someone that is under you to talk to you. He can, He is God. God used a donkey to talk to a prophet. It can be horizontally; you can get an instruction from God from your peers. Then obviously it can be upward vertical. When God uses someone in a community to give you an instruction, mostly it is not something that's totally new to you. What happens is that when that person tells you, it is as if that person gives you permission to act on it.

I picked up a sport some time ago, tennis. One day I went to the tennis court with my ball machine. The idea is to hit three hundred balls with my fore hand and three hundred balls with my back hand. So, practice mode was activated, the machine started shooting balls at me. I was hitting the forehand and I was hitting the backhand. But you see the forehand was going very well and the backhand not so well. After a while, I would hit the forehand and instead of hitting the backhand, I will turn around and hit another forehand. The forehand was going in and I kind of enjoy when things go in. I hit the forehand then turn around and hit the backhand. I felt very good with myself. So, I pick the balls, load them into the machine and then I go again. One security guard had been watching me from a distance, but I really did not notice him. When it was time to play the last one hundred and fifty balls, he said, "Sir, can I give you one advice?" In my mind I thought, "Okay? Here we go!" But I encouraged him to speak nonetheless. He said, "You have been hitting with your forehand and you are better at it already. But you have not really hit any balls with your backhand. My advice is that you stop hitting with your forehand and hit the balls with your backhand". Did I not know that already? I did but it took someone else to tell me, and when he told me, it was like he was giving me permission to do what I already knew I should do. Guess what happened? The last one hundred and fifty balls, I focused on hitting with my backhand. Initially, it was not going in but after like thirty balls, the balls began to fly in. I left that place with a stronger backhand because I listened to a security guard that had never played tennis all his life.

Some people are so head strong and arrogant, it is unbelievable. You cannot take instructions from the people above you not to talk of someone that you consider far from you. Meanwhile the solution to your life may just be with that someone that you consider far from you. I left that court a stronger player that day. The people that would typically beat me on the game still beat me, but the game was tougher because I had a stronger backhand. The people I used to struggle to beat, I began to beat them easily because I had a stronger backhand. The point is this, I could have pleased myself, ignored my weakness, and remained on the same level. Or I could listen to the voice of the community. There are people that God has put in your life to speak into your life so that you can become stronger. When you take instructions, you are doing yourself a favour because you are the one that becomes stronger.

In war, instruction is everything, intelligence is everything, line of command is everything. This may be the last chapter in this book, but it will open you up to so many new chapters in your journey to victory. There are only four ways you can change, only four ways you can move to the next level:

1. You can **do more**. [What should you do more?]
2. You can **do less**. [What should you do less?]
3. You can **stop**. [What should you stop doing?]
4. You can **start**. [What should you start doing?]

Now, do you remember the key people you penned down on your list for contribution earlier? Great, now I want you to take a bold step and ask them these four questions that are rooted in our four ways to move to the next level. Ask, what should I do less? Maybe I talk too much, and I need to talk less. Ask, what should I do more? Maybe I am an excellent cook, and I need to cook more. Ask, what should I stop? Maybe I spend too much of your time in front of the television. Then ask, what should I start? [What am I not doing?] These four questions will change your life. If you ask sincerely and humbly enough, and they tell you, it will change your life totally. Eat the humble pie and ask.

At the church I pastor (God's Favourite House), we always ask these four questions. We ask everyone that is new in church and get answers these four questions. What are we doing that we should stop doing? What are we doing that we should not stop doing? What are we doing that we should do more [or continue]? What are we doing that we should do less? We always ask because we recognize that new people have a fresher outlook and very often, they can see what we cannot see. If you want to take your life forward, ask those four questions.

When you practice the principle of concerted action, in addition to the other principles, you become totally unstoppable. You would be an enigma, you would be wonder to many. If you will do them, you will become totally unstoppable. Remember that at the beginning of this chapter, we said that the presence of Jesus gives us the supernatural benefit of synergy on fire. Josh.23:[10] (NLT) *"Each one of you will put to flight a thousand of the enemy..."* Why would you be able to put to flight a thousand? *"...for the **LORD** your God fights for you, just as he has promised."* God wants to fight for you but for God to fight for you, you must be on God's side. I have giving you this invitation repeatedly in the pages of this book, chapter after chapter. But I am handing you this invite again, you need God to fight for you and for this to happen, you need to be on God's side. It is just between you and God, Jesus is here, standing at the door and knocking. Open the door of your heart to Him and your victories will be unstoppable.

Finally, I want you to pray and ask God to help you stop doing the things that are repelling covenant relationships from your life. Ask God to help you start doing the things that will enable you to connect to the covenant relationships that He has for you. Ask God to help you reduce the things that you need to do less. Ask God to help you to consistently do the things that you need to more. I pray that God will help you stop doing the things that are repelling covenant relationships. I pray that God will empower you start doing the things you need to do to attract covenant relationships. I pray that God will empower you to do less of the things you need to do less and do more of the things you need to do more, in Jesus Name.

"In war there is no substitute for victory." – General Douglas MacArthur

Go and win!